# Contents

# Putting Research into Practice in Primary Teaching and Learning

Edited by

Suzi Clipson-Boyles

**David Fulton Publishers**

London

David Fulton Publishers Ltd
Ormond House, 26–27 Boswell Street, London WC1N 3JD
www.fultonbooks.co.uk

First published in Great Britain by David Fulton Publishers 2000

Note: The right of the Suzi Clipson-Boyles to be identified as the editor of this work has been asserted by her in accordance with the Copyright, Designs and Patents Act 1988.

Copyright © David Fulton Publishers 2000

*British Library Cataloguing in Publication Data*
A catalogue record for this book is available from the British Library

ISBN 1–85346–642–5

Typeset by Kate Williams, Abergavenny
Printed in Great Britain by The Cromwell Press Ltd, Trowbridge, Wilts.

# Notes on contributors

**Jonathan Allen**   Jonathan is a senior lecturer for ICT in Education at the School of Education, Oxford Brookes University. He has experience in both the primary and secondary sectors and is involved in a range of courses in the School of Education, primarily related to initial teacher education. Jonathan's main research interest is children's perception of ICT – a viewpoint not available to him as a child!

**Diana Bentley**   Diana is a freelance language consultant. Previously, she worked for six years researching the value and impact of primary reading resources at Reading University. She has written many books for teachers and children and is currently a consultant to *The Catch Up Project* at the School of Education, Oxford Brookes University. Her special area of interest is working with children who find reading difficult.

**Sonia Blandford**   Sonia is the Deputy Head of the School of Education at Oxford Brookes University and course leader of the EdD (Doctorate in Education). She has published several books on education management and professional development, focusing on the relationship of the management of teaching to learning.

**Michael Brown**   Michael is a senior lecturer at the School of Education, Oxford Brookes University where he is leader of the Primary PGCE course. He teaches geographical education on undergraduate, postgraduate and in-service training courses, and is currently engaged in research into children's understanding of landscape.

**Chris Carpenter**   Chris is Head of Physical Education at Wheatley Park School in Oxfordshire. He is currently working part-time as PE Advisory Teacher to Primary Schools. He is interested in all aspects of curriculum development in PE and has had a number of articles published in national journals and presented a paper on assessment in PE at the British Association of Advisers and Lecturers in Physical Education (BAALPE) annual conference.

**Suzi Clipson-Boyles**   Suzi is a principal lecturer at the School of Education, Oxford Brookes University where she is Project Director of *The Catch Up Project*, a national research and resource development project for Key Stage 2 literacy intervention. She also writes widely in the fields of primary english and drama. Her two main areas of research interest are the changing intervention needs for struggling readers in different year groups, and the impact of educational drama on disaffected pupils.

**Alan Cross**   Alan is Director of the Centre for Primary Education at the Department of Education, University of Manchester, where he leads the department's Primary PGCE course and teaches science and technology. He researches in the area of primary teaching method and has written widely in the areas of primary science and technology. He has contributed to a number of overseas programmes and given papers at international conferences. Alan also works as a consultant to LEAs and schools and is an OFSTED Team Inspector.

**Penny Fowler**   Penny is a principal lecturer at the School of Education, Oxford Brookes University where she has responsibility for initial teacher training. She teaches art education on undergraduate, postgraduate and in-service training courses. She previously taught art in two other higher education settings. Penny is a practising artist (painter) and has had several highly acclaimed one-person shows.

**Mary Kellett**   Mary is currently engaged in Special Educational Needs doctoral research at the School of Education, Oxford Brookes University. She was formerly a music coordinator in a primary school, and still sees herself as 'first and foremost a teacher'! Her special areas of interest are curricular access for the less able, non-threatening approaches to the music curriculum, assisting the non-specialist music teacher, and the musically disaffected pupil.

**Deborah Lucas**   Deborah is a chartered educational psychologist working independently in Bath and North-East Somerset. She currently works with families, and is supporting a local primary school committed to the development of inclusion. Her special area of interest is systems work.

**David Mancey**   David is a senior lecturer at the School of Education, Oxford Brookes University where his work is mainly in primary science. He links science and the environment not only in his university teaching but also in his work with outside organisations. His research interests include the development of ecological ideas in individuals of different ages.

**Nick Mead**   Nick is senior lecturer in religious education at Westminster College, Oxford where he has also introduced a Citizenship Elective into the college programme. He is a member of the Teacher Training Agency's Working Party on Pastoral and Relationships Education in ITT. His areas of research are the relationship between religious education and citizenship and the mentoring of religious education trainee specialists in primary and secondary schools.

**Alison Price**　Alison is a senior lecturer at the School of Education, Oxford Brookes University where she teaches primary mathematics education. She is interested in children's early mathematical development, and in particular their social and linguistic understanding as they learn mathematics. Her current research is into the learning of early arithmetic in Reception and Year One classes.

**Dee Reid**　Dee is a freelance lecturer leading courses and INSET across the UK, and is also currently a consultant to *The Catch Up Project* at Oxford Brookes University. Dee has published widely, most recently including 'Storyworlds', a new reading scheme for Heinemann, and 'Literacy Probe', a diagnostic test for seven- to nine-year-olds published by Hodder and Stoughton. Her special area of interest is working with children who find reading difficult.

**Gary Thomas**　Gary holds a Chair in Education at the School of Education, Oxford Brookes University. Previously he taught and researched at the University of the West of England and at University College London. He has directed research for a number of organisations including the DfEE, Barnados and the Nuffield Foundation and he currently holds a Leverhulme Research Fellowship. His most recent book *The Making of the Inclusive School* won the TES/NASEN Book of the Year Award in 1998.

**Peter Vass**　Peter is a senior lecturer at the School of Education, Oxford Brookes University where he teaches history education. He spent many years working in primary and middle schools where he was involved in a variety of research projects. He has written many articles on the teaching and learning of history and his current research interest is on the role of narrative plays in young children's understanding of that subject.

# Foreword

In recent years evidence-based practice has come to be seen as fundamental to the delivery of effective services in the helping professions. Being aware of the efficacy of different approaches to professional practice, understanding the theoretical underpinnings of different ways of working and applying a research-based model of enquiry to analysing problems have all come to be seen as characteristics of the thoughtful practitioner and maximally effective service delivery.

In education this approach has not been as widely or as warmly embraced as it has in other fields. I suspect that there are a number of reasons for this. To begin with, educational researchers and educational research have not always addressed the problems of classroom practice or school systems in ways that have appeared meaningful to teachers and educational managers. Equally, teachers for a long time were neither trained nor encouraged to undertake research and all too often have not had the skills to interpret or apply the findings of researchers. Communication, too, has been a problem. Researchers have often been guilty of writing in obscure language in journals inaccessible to teachers. Teachers, on the other hand, faced with the demands of the classroom have little time to read and reflect; a problem that has been exacerbated by the decreasing opportunities which are available for them to gain release from school to undertake in-service education let alone become involved in research themselves, even in their own classroom.

The idea of the 'teacher as reflective practitioner' and work which has been produced by 'teachers as researchers' has produced an increasing awareness of the importance of the relationship which can and should exist between research and practice. The need to bring research and practice into a dynamic association has been increasingly recognised along with the importance of links between theory and practice and the establishment of partnerships between colleagues in higher education and in schools.

This book will undoubtedly help teachers and trainee teachers to recognise the potential value of these links. The aim of the book is to close the gap between research and practice and each chapter outlines outcomes of research which can be applied practically in the classroom. It highlights the accessibility of research by writing about its relevance with a clear focus on the provision of high quality teaching and learning. The book also breaks new ground in that it goes beyond the normal presentation of research findings by providing photocopiable key resource materials at the end of each chapter which demonstrate how practical ideas for teaching can be developed from research findings.

In sum this is no 'dusty' research volume. Rather it 'dares to be different' by stressing the utility of research and paving the way for a more professional and practical approach to using research in the classroom.

Graham Upton

Vice Chancellor, Oxford Brookes University

January 2000

*Chapter 1*

# Introduction

*Suzi Clipson-Boyles*

## Using this book

This book is written for primary teachers, head teachers and trainee teachers who are unfamiliar with the world of educational research and would like to know more. It is hoped that it will encourage more practitioners to become everyday users of research as well as assisting those who are interested in conducting their own classroom studies. It aims to make useful links between research and primary classroom practice by examining focus studies for each area of the primary curriculum, including drama, RE, special needs and education management. It does not seek to provide comprehensive reviews of subject areas, but aims to demonstrate how practitioners might develop their thinking and classroom practice in response to research findings about specific aspects relating to each subject area. These translations of findings into practice are exemplified through photocopiable link resource sheets, one for each chapter, offering practical ideas and activities that have been designed in response to the research described.

The book is intended as a starting point for using education research by providing:

- an introductory overview of current issues in educational research;
- an introduction to basic research terminology;
- examples of how the authors have used the research of others to develop their own thinking about classroom practice;
- examples of how the authors have used their own research to develop their thinking about classroom practice;
- suggestions on how to access further research;
- a focus point for each subject area that teachers might use to develop their own action research or further reading; and
- practical suggestions that might be followed up and developed further in the classroom.

## Research and practice: bridging the gap

The spirit of this book is about building bridges between educational research and the everyday work of teachers in primary classrooms. In the past, these two cultures have been distinctly separate, research all too often being perceived as the exclusive domain of academics working in universities. Exclusivity, inaccessibility and, in many cases, academic elitism have all been features of educational research in the past, and arguably these have created barriers to important findings reaching the very people who need them. Interest in educational research has usually been limited to particular stake holders, for example government, funding agencies and research agencies. In universities there has been a tendency for educational research activities to be conducted by a minority of academics, and sometimes their work has seemed far removed from the practicalities and everyday realities of actual education in practice. Indeed, even today, many education lecturers responsible for the training of teachers are so heavily involved in course development, teaching, assessment and administration that there is little or no time left for writing and research.

Likewise, teachers, head teachers and those working in local education authorities (LEAs) have felt themselves to be outside, or separate from the research community. There are, of course, some notable exceptions. For instance there have been research and statistics centres within some LEAs that have provided exemplary models of good practice in the way their findings have fed back into local policy development and schools' decision-making. Also, the recent growth in professional research degrees combined with the development of action research and reflective practitioner models have meant that more teachers now feel that they have an ownership of research knowledge and practice. But it is also true to say that classrooms have been predominantly the sites for, rather than the beneficiaries of, research in the vast majority of cases. So why does this situation exist, when our common sense tells us that much of what is produced by educational researchers might make a difference to teaching and learning? There are three apparent reasons for the divide that are closely interlinked.

### *Lack of relevance*

Firstly, research has not always seemed relevant to the classroom practitioner. There has tended to be a fragmented approach to research planning that has generated massive quantities of unrelated projects. The consequence of this is a lack of theory building through the accumulated knowledge of related or replicated studies, which would strengthen our existing knowledge. In some cases, studies on more obscure topics, although of interest and importance to the researchers, do not always appear to connect directly with classroom practice in ways that might make a difference to teaching and learning. That is not to say that small-scale, or minority interest studies should not exist. Indeed, they add to the rich multi-dimensionality of the educational research culture and, providing the limits on generalisability are understood, they can have much to offer. However, it is also true to say that there is a gap at the other end of the scale, with insufficient generalisable research to inform policy and practice. Likewise, the links between research and development have been weak. All too often studies end, and the findings are left in a vacuum, the 'so what?' or 'what next?' factors failing to be addressed. This relates closely to the second reason for the research and practice divide.

### Restrictive dissemination practices

Research has not always been disseminated in ways that are readable, accessible and usable to teachers. Full research reports are, of course, essential if studies are to be checked and replicated. Likewise, academic journals have an important part to play because the peer review process through which articles are scrutinised (before publication is approved or rejected) provides a systematic quality assurance process. However, the problem has been that many academics have fallen short of disseminating beyond this point. Some have argued that the Research Assessment Exercise (RAE; see Glossary) is to blame for this, the research being driven by the need to score points for funding rather than the needs of teachers and learners in the classroom. However, the fact remains that if a study is likely to be of interest and use to teachers, researchers have an ethical duty to ensure that it is disseminated for that audience, for example through professional publications, the development of resources and in-service training events. Indeed, it can be argued that planning for this should be included at the very start of the process when applying for funding, if we are to be truly accountable for the impact of our work (although clearly the actual outcomes will not be clear until the study is complete).

### Divided communities

The third reason for the divide has been that research has been located as a separate activity or culture. In the past, teachers have rarely been consulted on what needs researching; they have been the subjects of studies rather than the instigators. It is unreasonable to expect all teachers to become researchers, although the reflective practitioner model is certainly something that all should adopt. However, it is perhaps time to consider other options that could strengthen the effectiveness of educational research. For instance, consultation partnerships when planning research, in-service dissemination of research, franchising of research among many individual schools linked by a coordinating researcher in the LEA or university, and so on. In other words, consultation and communication need to be considerably improved.

## The changing culture of educational research

It is against this background that educational research is currently undergoing dramatic changes that offer exciting new opportunities and challenges for those working in education. These changes are probably due to four significant factors.

### Teachers want research!

The recognition among a growing number of teachers that research can be relevant and useful to their everyday work means that there are greater expectations of researchers.

Researchers now have to be more accountable for the quality of their work, and have a responsibility to report it appropriately.

### The government wants research!

There has been a major shift by the present government towards developing evidence-based policy and practice at all levels. This is reflected by the commissioning and dissemination of research by the various education agencies, and the emphasis on teacher involvement. The government is also setting up systems to improve the sharing and communication of studies by extending the current research community into a more holistic and inclusive framework.

### The research community is changing

For some time now, there has been a growing and vigorous debate taking place within the community of researchers about the quality, remoteness and cost-effectiveness of educational research (see Carnine 1995; Bassey 1996, 1997; Budge 1996; Hargreaves 1996). This has started to extend to other commentators such as Her Majesty's Chief Inspector of Schools, the Teacher Training Agency (TTA) and the Department for Education and Employment (DfEE). News items have also meant that the debate is also starting to reach the ears of teachers! Two reviews took place in 1998 to investigate the state of educational research in Britain. One was commissioned by the Office for Standards in Education (OFSTED) (Tooley and Darby 1998) and the other by the DfEE; the latter was undertaken by the Institute for Employment Studies (Hillage *et al.* 1998). Although very different in character and methodology, both studies found that educational research was currently having little impact on, or relevance to, policy and practice (although it was agreed that this is an extremely difficult thing to isolate and measure). These two reports make interesting reading and should be studied closely by all who are interested in the current debate.

### Changing research practices

There is an ever increasing diversity of approaches to research methods and methodologies. Some, particularly those who are committed to a very specific paradigm, see this as problematic. Others see this as tremendously beneficial because it means that education is being examined in different ways from a rich variety of perspectives, which gives a multifaceted picture of what is happening in schools. In the early days of educational research, traditional scientific methods (quantitative) were usually used to measure specific variables that could be isolated (e.g. intelligence, reading age, etc.). However, some would argue that the social nature of education renders it almost impossible to isolate variables in the way that scientists might do in a laboratory. This resulted in the growth of more ethnographic approaches, which created what is still sometimes called the quantitative/qualitative divide. In reality, each of these categories can be further subdivided into a fascinating number of different approaches. Many researchers (although by no means all) are starting to recognise that rather than competing, the two paradigms can be mutually beneficial. Scientific checks can ensure that we are not making unrepresentative claims, and ethnographic insights can add more depth to otherwise two-dimensional number-crunching. The debate about approach is important, but it is underpinned by the equally significant argument about quality. Unbiased sampling, triangulation, clear descriptions of method and methodology and transparent selection of data for reporting are all required if objectivity and integrity are to be assured. And even in more personal studies where subjectivity is part of what is being explored, that should be clear to the reader. (Details of terminology are provided in the Glossary if required.)

This new culture offers tremendous scope for positive change and development as the ownership of research shifts towards a more inclusive framework. An important theme running through this book is the implications of this for teaching and learning.

## Why do teachers need research?

Every day, teachers constantly make decisions that affect the learners in their classrooms. Those decisions are influenced by many factors: school policies; government legislative frameworks; parental expectations; what has worked in the past; what is realistic within the practical context of the classroom; and what is permitted by the availability of resources, to name but a few.

However, it is also important for teachers' decisions to be informed by a professional knowledge of what works – evidence-based practice. In other words it is important to know not just *what* to teach and *how* to teach it, but also *why* one decision might be better than another. Theoretical bases that are grounded in reliable evidence can provide sound foundations for both long-term planning and everyday decisions. So how can primary teachers become 'interested parties', and in doing so feel an ownership of educational research by being very much a part of that research community? A minority of teachers like to engage in research themselves, and this is adding a new dimension to the way schools use and regard research. However, it is perhaps even more important to develop a culture where all teachers become regular users of research.

### *Some teacher-friendly routes to useful research*

The recognition that educational research should be more accessible to teachers has meant that it is now more usual for professional publications to include relevant and useful items. The monthly magazines *Primary* (*Times Educational Supplement*) and *Junior Education* (Scholastic) for instance, both have research news sections, with descriptions of new studies and information on how to access further details if required. There are also organisations that offer useful research support, services and information.

#### *The British Educational Research Association (BERA)*
This association was established in 1974, its aims being to encourage 'the pursuit of educational research and its application for the improvement of educational practice and the general benefit of the community'. It produces the *British Educational Research Journal* (*BERJ*) and a newsletter, *Research Intelligence,* both of which are included in the subscrip-

tion price. It also organises local and national courses, workshops and debates, and an annual conference. For details, write to:

> BERA Office
> c/o Scottish Council for Research in Education
> 15 St John Street
> Edinburgh EH8 8JR

*DfEE research briefs*
Research commissioned by the DfEE is disseminated in two ways: the full report is usually available in booklet form, and short summary sheets called research briefs provide the main details and findings. Lists of available reports can be obtained from:

> DfEE Publications
> PO Box 5050
> Sudbury           Tel: 0845 60 22260
> Suffolk CO10 6ZQ   Email: dfee@prologistics.co.uk

*The National Foundation for Educational Research (NFER)*
Set up in 1946, the NFER undertakes research into all aspects of educational practice and is funded through research contracts, a grant from the Council of LEAs and income from NFER-Nelson. It produces an extremely useful quarterly newsletter to those on its mailing list, reports of research, publications arising from research and the very useful research information sheets, which provide summary information with contact names for fuller reports and further details if required.

> Tel: 01753 574123           Website: http://www.nfer.ac.uk

*OFSTED*
OFSTED produces reports based on inspection data, and also commissions research from time to time to support and inform its work. These can be obtained from:

> OFSTED
> Alexandra House
> 33 Kingsway
> London WC2B 6SE    Tel: 0171 421 6800

*The TTA Teacher Research Grant Scheme*
The TTA provides small grants for teachers who wish to conduct research in their own schools and classrooms. These studies are disseminated in short reports, available from:

> The Teacher Research Grant Scheme
> Teacher Training Agency
> Portland House
> Stag Place          Publications line: 0845 606 0323
> London SWJE 5TT      Website: www.teach-tta.gov.uk

## How this book is organised

The chapters offer an interesting variety of levels of research, ranging from the author's own studies to the impact of policy research. Some authors have focused on one study in detail, whereas others have discussed a group of several related studies. The chapters, brief descriptions of which are provided here, are organised in the following order:

- cross-curricular subjects;
- the three core subjects; and
- other subjects (alphabetically).

### *Education management*

*Chapter 2, Managing positive behaviour*
Sonia Blandford aims to deepen teachers' and head teachers' understanding of the management of positive behaviour in schools by describing a study where the emphasis was on the relationship between need and management.

Link resource: Target book (repeated page), for teachers and pupils to set daily targets and record achievements relating to behaviour.

### *Special needs*

*Chapter 3, Organising classrooms to promote learning for all children: two pieces of action research*
Deborah Lucas and Gary Thomas describe two action research projects in which teachers planned for the special educational needs of children through changing the organisation and geography of their classrooms.

Link resource: Classroom planning grid, to assist with classroom organisation of tasks and supporting roles.

### *English*

*Chapter 4, Catching up with reading: from classroom research to national project*
Diana Bentley and Dee Reid explain how the findings of various research studies were used to develop an intervention programme for struggling readers.

Link resource: Reading attitude questionnaire, to help teachers find out about children's perceptions of, and attitudes towards reading.

### *Maths*

*Chapter 5, Reading and writing arithmetic*
Alison Price looks at three main areas of research into how children use symbols. She goes on to describe how teachers can help children move from working in arithmetic mentally to recording their work and making sense of the recordings of others.

Link resource: Maths writing frame, for children to record problem-solving activities.

## Science

*Chapter 6, Science: the need for an environmental focus*
David Mancey explains how findings about children's understanding of the natural environment can be used to help plan effective science teaching in the primary school.

Link resource: Group discussion recording sheet – a framework to guide children through, and help them record, science discussions.

## Art

*Chapter 7, An antidote for diffidence in teaching art to children at Key Stage 2*
Penny Fowler is concerned about the effects that teacher diffidence can have on art provision. She offers a solution that has been developed through her own ongoing reflective research into this area.

Link resource: My private encounters with art – a personal reflective activity for teachers and students to privately assess their own feelings about art and art teaching.

## Design and technology

*Chapter 8, Design and technology: raising the profile of teaching method*
Alan Cross seeks to characterise good teaching in design and technology by reviewing how research has highlighted effective pedagogical approaches to this subject.

Link resource: Teaching methods checklist, for teachers to consult when planning design and technology sessions.

## Drama

*Chapter 9, Developing language and literacy through drama*
This chapter focuses on how drama can enhance the teaching of language and literacy by describing studies relating to oracy, reading and writing. A case is made for using drama activities during the Literacy Hour.

Link resource: Hot-seating flow chart, to help teachers plan hot-seating activities as a means of exploring texts.

## Geography

*Chapter 10, Understanding, making and using maps*
Mike Brown reviews some of the seminal work on how children develop their conceptual thinking about maps and discusses how this can help teachers to plan appropriate activities. He then goes on to use this existing research knowledge to develop a proposed developmental framework of mapping abilities at Key Stage 1.

Link resource: Mapping stairway – a checklist of skills against which teachers can track and plan for children's progression through three developmental levels of understanding.

## History

*Chapter 11, Telling the truth? Using stories to teach history to young children*
Peter Vass describes his own research into the outcomes of telling then discussing stories with young children as a means of helping them to distinguish historical facts from fiction.

Link resource: Questions to ask after story-telling, to provide a guide for teachers to questioning with a history focus.

## Information and communications technology

*Chapter 12, Information and communications technology: investigating new frontiers*
Jonathan Allen ventures into the relatively new area of ICT research and focuses particularly on that which explores the development of children's word processing skills.

Link resource: Word processing skills planning checklist, to assist teachers with the planning of word processing skills.

## Music

*Chapter 13, Motivating the musically disaffected*
Mary Kellett describes and discusses a project in which special activities and teaching approaches were designed for children who were disaffected with music. These resulted in improved listening skills and higher musical self-esteem.

Link resource: Pattern designs, to provide children with the visual stiumli required for a musical activity described in the chapter.

## Physical education

*Chapter 14, Demystifying the core strands in the National Curriculum for physical education*
Chris Carpenter describes two studies that investigate teachers' perceptions about the relationship between planning, performance and evaluation in PE. He goes on to describe how an integrated approach to teaching the three areas can help overcome teachers' fears and also maximise children's learning.

Link resource: Teacher checklist, to help teachers reflect on the types of approaches they are using in PE.

## Religious education

*Chapter 15, Researching skills common to religious education and citizenship*
Nick Mead focuses on the processes that teachers can use to make valuable links between RE and citizenship, by looking at research that examines what is common to both.

Link resource: Staff self-assessment exercise and skills audit for the teaching of RE and citizenship, to assist discussion in a training or policy planning meeting

## Useful further reading

*Research Methods in Education*, Louis Cohen and Lawrence Manion (1994). London: Routledge.

A useful and comprehensive practical guide to a wide range of research approaches. Each of the 16 chapters deals with a different aspect, not only explaining the developmental and/or theoretical background but also providing a guide to how practitioners might consider using these approaches.

*Effective Primary Teaching: research-based classroom strategies*, Paul Croll and Nigel Hastings (eds) (1997). London: David Fulton Publishers.

An excellent book that provides teachers with reviews of the collected research about effective teaching. It describes strategies that should be considered in the light of evidence that they will make a significant difference to teaching and learning in primary classrooms.

*Taking the Fear Out of Data Analysis*, Adamantios Diamantopoulos and Bodo B. Schlegelmilch (1997). London: The Dryden Press.

These authors really understand what it is to be frightened of numbers! This book takes you on a logical and thorough journey through the minefield of data, using clear explanations and useful examples. Helpful to those planning research and those who need help deciphering the maths!

*Qualitative Data Analysis*, Matthew B. Miles and A. Michael Huberman (1994). Thousand Oaks, CA: Sage Publications.

This is a must for teachers who may be planning their own qualitative study, for example an MEd or EdD dissertation or action research project. Each chapter takes you through the stages of analysis, outlining rationale, procedure and problems. A practical guide with a sound academic underpinning.

*Statistics Without Tears: a primer for non-mathematicians*, Derek Rowntree (1981). London: Penguin.

This book is brilliant for those who lack confidence with numbers. It can be a useful reference book when reading reports based on heavily quantitative data, and is also of great assistance to those designing studies that will require statistical analysis.

*Understanding Educational Research*, David Scott and Robin Usher (eds) (1996). London: Routledge.

This book looks at the relationship between the nature of knowledge, methodology and practice, and in particular describes new research paradigms that are emerging in the contemporary education research culture.

*Researching Education,* David Scott and Robin Usher (1999). London: Cassell.

This book discusses philosophy, strategies, methods and issues. As such it raises some challenging questions about the nature of research and its involvement with the operation of power.

# References

Bassey, M. (1996) 'We are specialists at pursuing the truth', *Times Educational Supplement,* 22 November.

Bassey, M. (1997) 'Annual expenditure on educational research in the UK', *Research Intelligence* **59**, February, 2–3.

Budge, D. (1996) 'A cosy world of trivial pursuits?', *Times Educational Supplement,* 28 June.

Carnine, D. (1995) 'Trustworthiness, usability and accessibility of educational research', *Journal of Behavioural Education* **5**(3).

Hargreaves, D. (1996) 'Teaching as a research-based profession: possibilities and prospects' The Teacher Training Agency Annual Lecture. London: HMSO.

Hillage, J. *et al.* (1998) *Excellence in Research on Schools.* Sudbury: DfEE Publications.

Tooley, J. and Darby, D. (1998) *Educational Research: A Critique.* London: OFSTED.

# Chapter 2

# Managing positive behaviour

*Sonia Blandford*

At a time when teachers and other professionals are increasingly worried about reported increases in antisocial behaviour in schools there is a need to identify real needs and provide real solutions to the management of positive behaviour.

In this chapter I focus on two years' qualitative research based on observations and interviews with teachers and support agencies in a range of schools in England. The aim is to deepen the understanding of the management of positive behaviour in schools, encompassing internal and external support agencies, with an emphasis on the relationship between need and management. The chapter provides practical support for teachers, managers and other professionals involved in the promotion of positive behaviour in schools.

## Introduction

Defining behaviour sounds easy. It is a term frequently used by practitioners, members of the school community and society in general. Whether there is a shared meaning is doubtful, as the range of behaviours and attitudes regarded as disruptive and requiring discipline is vast. In practice, any definition, and subsequent interpretation of behaviour, will reflect the beliefs and values of all members of the school community. Where there is no shared understanding, tensions will exist and possibly crises will occur.

It is axiomatic that the promotion of positive behaviour is central to effective teaching and learning. If teachers are unable to manage a class, they will be unable to teach. Consistency is a fundamental problem in educational practice, as there are so many variables that influence teaching and learning. All teachers are responsible, as professionals, for promoting positive behaviour in schools. Critical to practice is the relationship between teachers, pupils, parents (and families), senior management, governors, local education authority support agencies, educationalists and central government.

The wholly incorrect assumption that promoting positive behaviour implies 'doing something to someone' reflects the needs of those who like to control members of the school community. Effective and lasting behaviour management focuses on the ability of individuals to manage themselves: self-discipline. If all members of the school community were self-disciplined individuals there would be very few, if any, behaviour problems.

The outward manifestation of the ability of individuals to either behave in an acceptable manner (self-control) or have discipline thrust upon them (control) is displayed in their attitude and behaviour towards others and their environment. The boundaries of acceptable behaviour should allow schools to function as harmonious and humane communities in order to create an environment conducive to serious learning (Docking 1980). Where boundaries are accepted, pupils will have the self-control to manage their behaviour and attitudes without authority figures. So if it is agreed that positive behaviour is concerned with the development of internal mechanisms that enable individuals to control themselves, there will need to be agreed boundaries for attitudes and behaviour. The promotion of positive behaviour in schools is the responsibility of all members of the school community. Individuals need to know and understand what is acceptable to other members of the community.

In order for there to be a shared understanding, all members of the school community need to participate in the decision-making process leading to the publication of a behaviour policy. Central government, past and present, has recognised the need for schools to maintain a disciplined environment that is safe and secure for all pupils and teachers, yet discipline is rarely mentioned in the context of education reform. In practice, legislation has been created to deal with problem pupils (Education Act 1993), and guidance for teachers is provided in the report of the Committee of Enquiry chaired by Lord Elton, entitled *Discipline in Schools* (Department of Education and Science (DES) 1989), and in the Department for Education (DfE) circular, *Pupil Behaviour and Discipline* (DfE 1994b).

The Elton Committee was established by the Secretary of State for Education and Science in March 1988. The Elton Report provided guidance to senior management teams and classroom teachers through recommendations that the committee believed would secure a real improvement in all schools. The committee found that there were no simple or complete remedies because discipline is a complex issue. Critically, they recognised the importance of clearly stated boundaries of acceptable behaviour, and of teachers responding promptly and firmly to pupils who test those boundaries.

The report concluded that helping teachers to become effective classroom managers could reduce the central problem of disruption. The importance of initial and in-service training courses was highlighted, particularly the need for initial teacher training (ITT) courses to include specific practical training related to motivating and managing pupils, and dealing with those who challenge authority. The committee suggested that in-service courses should aim to refine classroom management skills and to develop patterns of mutual support among colleagues.

Further recommendations included head teachers and senior management teams taking a lead in developing school plans for promoting good behaviour. The committee considered that the head teacher's management style was a critical factor in encouraging a sense of collective responsibility among staff and a sense of commitment to the school among pupils and their parents.

The quality of the school environment was also deemed to be important, as was the atmosphere or ethos of the school. The report suggested that the most effective schools were those with the best relationships with parents. The school's discipline policy should be communicated fully and clearly to parents. The committee also advised that parents have a responsibility to provide their children with firm guidance and positive models through their own behaviour. The importance of parent–teacher associations was highlighted as a means of creating both formal and informal channels of communication about behaviour. The report concluded that there was a need to increase parental accountability for children's behaviour. The report suggested that children were also to be encouraged to take more responsibility for their own and their peers' behaviour.

The committee recommended that LEAs should make provision for cost-effective support services for schools and individual children. It suggested that the most effective provision would be based on support teams of specialist teachers working in mainstream schools, with access to places in on-site and (as appropriate) off-site units. The committee stressed the need for rapid assessment by all LEAs of the special educational needs of children with emotional and behavioural difficulties.

The report indicated that attendance rates were relatively stable and that any significant differences in the rates for individual schools could not always be explained by differences in catchment areas. The committee urged head teachers and teachers to act in order to minimise unauthorised absence and truancy. The committee also highlighted the importance of the school governing body, and particularly the head teacher, in the development and monitoring of the school discipline policy and appointment of staff.

The report urged LEAs to develop management information systems to target consultancy and support services for schools in difficulty. The committee believed that behaviour problems were sometimes associated with the use of supply teachers and recommended that steps should be taken to minimise their use. Interestingly, the report did not identify a relationship between class size and children's behaviour.

Having identified the need to tackle discipline in schools, the government focused on providing advice on a range of issues relating to pupil behaviour, emotional and behavioural difficulties, and the education of sick children. The six 1994 DfE circulars were concerned with:

- pupil behaviour and discipline (DfE 1994b);
- education of children with emotional and behavioural difficulties (with the Department of Health (DoH), DfE 1994c);
- exclusions from school (DfE 1994d);
- the education by LEAs of children otherwise than at school (DfE 1994e);
- the education of sick children (with the DoH, DfE 1994f); and
- the education of children being looked after by local authorities (DfE 1994g).

The circulars were intended to help schools maintain good behaviour and discipline based on good practice described in the Elton Report. Much of what was included in them reflected the government's emphasis on school leadership and the introduction of the National Curriculum. The circulars also provided invaluable guidance on the complexities of the Education Act 1993 and subsequent legislation. The following summaries are an introduction to circulars 8/94, 9/94 and 10/94 (DfE 1994b, c, d) and, as such, provide a framework for practice relating to post-Education Reform Act 1988 (ERA) policy and legislation.

Although the Elton Report and subsequent government circulars provided advice and guidance for practitioners, there was still a need to examine what was actually happening in schools. More recently the Standards Fund (DfEE 1998) has provided LEAs with the opportunity to bid for additional resources in order to tackle behaviour problems in schools. In addition the creation of educational action zones has focused government expenditure on those areas deemed to have the greatest need. To date, no evaluations of these initiatives have been published.

## Researching the management of behaviour

Having been employed as a middle manager and senior teacher in primary and secondary schools I developed a practical and theoretical interest in the promotion of positive behaviour in schools. On completion of a Doctorate in Education I was appointed lecturer in education management at Oxford Brookes University, which provided both the time and facilities to develop research activities. Following valued advice I was able to focus on an area of interest related to practical experience – the management of discipline in schools. The purpose of my research was to observe the management of behaviour in schools in order to develop a framework for practice.

The research began in 1996, focusing on practitioners at two levels: national and local. The national study was completed in the first year of the research, and involved telephone interviews and a postal survey of independent support agencies. The local study focused on one authority in the west of England known to me. The authority was selected on the basis of demographic diversity (urban, suburban and rural) and the range of practitioner expertise and experience available to me. The aim of both the local and national studies was to gather evidence of good practice in the management of behaviour in primary and secondary schools. The research question, 'How is positive behaviour managed in schools?', remained central to each phase of the study.

As a researcher I was able to shadow, observe and interview classroom teachers, managers, governors, parents, children, education welfare officers, LEA officers, educational psychologists, emotional and behavioural support teachers, learning support teachers, external agencies and behaviour coordinators. This provided invaluable data for analysis. I was also able to gather information through literature and alternative agencies that provided professional guidance for practitioners on related issues.

### *Findings*

Following the period of observation, data collection and literature search I concluded that the promotion of positive behaviour in schools is a complex area involving all members of the school and wider educational community. In schools where behaviour is a problem there is little chance of pupils receiving an education that meets their needs. If children are to develop academically, they also need to develop socially. Children need self-esteem and self-confidence in order to reach their potential as members of the school community. More specifically the research revealed the following:

- Teachers need to feel good about their practice. There is a tendency within education to criticise practice and, in doing so, belittle the professional status of practitioners. Good practice is not an imaginary phenomenon; it happens in most schools on a daily basis. There is much to be celebrated.
- Teachers should feel confident that they are able to provide a safe, secure environment in which children learn, adapting behaviour management policies to meet the needs of a pluralistic society. Yet, the researcher observed that the majority of practitioners encounter behaviour problems within their classrooms that are beyond their experience and expertise.

In order to address these issues I found that a framework for promoting positive behaviour would include:

- effective management;
- multi-agency support;
- pastoral responsibility; and
- teams.

### Effective management

The importance of effective management cannot be overstated. If schools are to adopt a multi-agency approach to the management of behaviour, there is a need to know and understand basic principles of education management. Teachers, support agencies and senior managers should develop the skills and abilities required for developing, implementing and managing effective behaviour strategies. Highly committed professionals are needed to ensure that schools create a sense of community and achieve their goals. Successful teachers and senior management teams manage successful schools. Effective management of positive behaviour does not just happen; it requires consultation, planning, commitment, and constant review and evaluation.

### Multi-agency support

A shared understanding of education management will enable schools to design, implement and review a behaviour policy that works within the school and reflects the needs of pupils, teachers, support agencies and the community.

The promotion of positive behaviour in schools has to be placed within the context of the management structures that exist at governmental, LEA and school levels. In essence, the promotion of positive behaviour in schools involves:

- teachers/senior managers;
- general assistants/school meal service assistants;
- parents;
- non-teaching support staff;
- governors;
- support agencies;
- education welfare officers/education officers/children's officers;
- support teams/social services;
- the LEA advisory service;
- educational psychologists;

- medical teams; and
- the judicial system and the police.

The extent to which each of the above is consulted depends on the child and the issue to be addressed. What is important is that in the matter of behaviour management, teachers should not feel isolated. The management structure of the school, all members of the school community as shown in Figure 2.1, should know the LEA and support agencies.

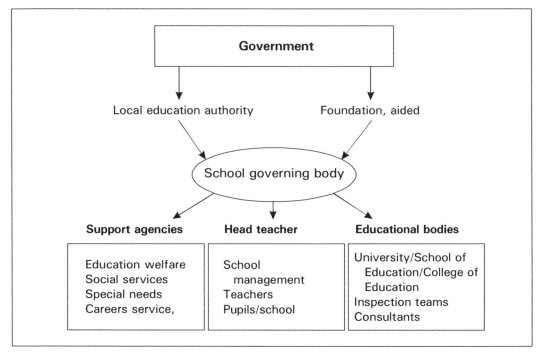

**Figure 2.1** School management – external agencies

*Pastoral responsibility*
I believe that every teacher has a pastoral responsibility for the children in their school. In practice this involves regular contact with parents, members of the community and external agencies in addition to the more formalised agencies within the local authority. Areas of responsibility need to be well defined within this often-neglected area of school management. There is a need to develop a system of pastoral care that:

- is workable;
- recognises the needs of the pupil;
- recognises the needs of the school;
- is understood and acknowledged by all staff (teaching and non-teaching);
- relates to the school's vision and school development plan;
- allows teachers to develop knowledge and understanding skills and abilities; and
- includes the management positive behaviour in continuing professional development and in-service education and training (INSET) programmes.

*Teams*

The management of teams within schools and the community is also a critical feature of effective behaviour management in schools. There are many features common to all school management teams, across all phases of education.

The supportive and caring element of teamwork is fundamental to the effective management of discipline in school. In any challenging and demanding situation, teachers need the security of belonging to a strong team. Effective management involves sharing the pressures created by difficult children. Teams do not act as teams simply because they are described as such. Teamwork means a group of people working together on the basis of:

- shared perceptions;
- a common purpose;
- agreed procedures;
- commitment;
- cooperation; and
- resolving disagreements openly by discussion.

As with the creation of the school identity, successful teamwork depends on a clearly defined set of aims and objectives, and the personalities of the team members and team manager. One function of all teams (multi-agency, pastoral, year and Key Stage) is to ensure that all members of the community have a shared understanding of how discipline will be managed within the school.

## Implications for teaching

A child has only one opportunity to receive compulsory education. Schools have a responsibility to ensure that they provide an effective curriculum delivered in a safe and secure environment. Any behaviour that challenges a child's ability to learn should be managed. Teachers and children need support systems to deal with difficulties with discipline. Equally, all teachers and children need to recognise the significance of their role within the school community. All members of the school community should feel respected, safe and able to participate in the daily routine of school life.

Teachers are contracted to teach. In order to do so they must be able to manage their classrooms. Their ability to maintain discipline will impact directly on their ability to teach. Teachers need to have the necessary knowledge and understanding of managing pupil behaviour before they enter the profession. When teachers require expert support and advice, this will need to be provided by a highly qualified and effective team of professional agencies. Communication is critical, as teachers need to know what is available to help them manage their classrooms effectively.

There are aspects of the culture of the teaching profession that militate against teachers being able to teach in an effective manner. Teachers are often wary of admitting that they have a difficulty with a particular class or pupil. This leads to tensions and pressure on all concerned. Teachers must be able to seek guidance and support when faced with the intolerable problem of disruptive behaviour in their classrooms. As professionals, teachers need to be able to discuss such problems with their colleagues and managers in an open, confident way. Fear of 'owning up' to a problem with discipline often leads teachers to experience severe stress, which causes inevitable damage to their health.

Classroom teachers need to manage behaviour in a caring, confident manner. They also need to be managed in a caring, confident manner. Managers should recognise the stresses caused by indiscipline in the classroom by providing practitioners with positive mechanisms for dealing with disruptive behaviour. This research revealed that in the weakest schools aspects of teaching and learning styles and curriculum development needed to be examined. An appropriate curriculum is critical to effective behaviour management.

### Target book

In my research I found that one of the most effective aids for monitoring behaviour and focusing children on how to learn was the use of a target book. This is appropriate for children aged 7 and over, and page 24 can be photocopied by readers who want to try this approach. The target book provides boundaries for the child and a reason for attending school. In two of the research schools I observed children asking for a target book. The gold-coloured book did much for the self-esteem of the pupils and teachers. Through the book individual needs were identified and met, teaching and learning took place and both children and their teachers gained respect.

The following children were observed using the target book to good effect:

- statemented children;
- children who had particular behavioural and/or learning difficulties; and
- children with a specific difficulty in any subject.

Use of the book was implemented in the following way:

- the children were identified, by teacher/parent/special needs coordinator/child;
- the head of year/head teacher was notified;
- the head of year/head teacher contacted the children's parents;
- targets were negotiated, by head of year or special needs coordinator, as appropriate;
- targets were monitored according to need; and
- parents were consulted prior to the introduction of the book and before the end of the target date.

The targets varied according to the nature and scope of the problem and were categorised as:

- special needs/cross-curricular
- behavioural/organisational; and
- subject-based.

*Special needs/cross-curricular – monitored by the class teacher*
- self-organisation
- task focused
- corrective reading
- spelling programme

*Behavioural/organisational – monitored by the class teacher/head of year/head teacher*
- lateness
- equipment
- relationships with peers
- bullying
- uniform

*Subject-based – monitored by the class teacher/head of year*
- concepts, understanding
- skills
- homework

The book begins with a clear set of instructions for each pupil (overleaf). The teacher is responsible for negotiating with the pupil on the most appropriate use of the book. (It was interesting to note that throughout this study I witnessed in children the desire to behave and learn; their problem was that they did not know how to!) The negotiated target will then be completed by the date agreed by the child, teacher(s) and parent/guardian. All information/negotiations were recorded on the child's action plan, which was retained by the head teacher in consultation with external agencies.

The target book contains:

- one page for each day;
- a clearly stated target;
- space for the teacher's comments at the end of each lesson;
- space for the child to add a comment;
- a homework section, with the date for the homework to be completed.

The book is A5 in size, giving ample space to record *all* information. It begins with a list of instructions for children that are clear and unambiguous (see Figure 2.2).

## Conclusions

Schools need to have a code by which members of their community can monitor their behaviour and attitude towards each other and their environment. Self-esteem and self-confidence are to be nurtured. Schools should allow individuals to develop and grow. This should happen within a collective framework based on shared beliefs and values. Teachers can create a positive environment by nurturing children's self-esteem. Encouragement and support are effective tools in the management of discipline. Children will respect boundaries that are understood and practised by all.

---

1. **You must:**
   - remember to bring your book to school every day and show your teacher;
   - remember to give your book to your class teachers at the start of every lesson, and they will then write a comment to help you;
   - remember to show your book to your parent/guardian every day.

2. **Targets will be:**
   - *negotiated* – between teachers and the child;
   - *clear* – understood and workable;
   - *goal orientated* – with achievable aims and measurable success;
   - *possible!* – able to be achieved by the child at home or at school;
   - *positive* – pupils and teachers must be able to identify any progress made;
   - *active* – do-able!;
   - *time-limited* – a time must be set and kept to.

3. **Success**
   - You and your teacher will know when you have reached your target.
   - When you have reached your target you can then move on to another one.
   - If you cannot reach your target a new one must be set.

   *This book is not a punishment. If used properly it will help you to learn.*

---

**Figure 2.2**   First page of Target book

School managers need to establish a regime that is firm and fair. The need for praise is as appropriate for teachers as it is for pupils. Praise and encouragement should be used as much as possible. Home–school contracts can be a useful mechanism if approached in a reasonable and consistent manner. Expectations must be achievable. Collaboration with members of the school community and support agencies is essential to good practice.

Multi-agency approaches to managing individual, group, class or whole-school behaviour issues should be adopted. This research has also shown that the expertise of education welfare officers, educational psychologists and support teachers for pupils with emotional and behavioural difficulties should be utilised in the development and implementation of behaviour management policies and strategies.

Communication is essential in the development and implementation of an effective discipline policy. Teachers and pupils should have a voice in the development of policy, procedures and practices. Relationships with everyone are critical. Teachers, managers and children need to relate to each other positively. Negative reactions to difficult situations will not lead to an early resolution; anger and confrontation should be avoided. Teachers need to monitor the levels of stress created in their classrooms.

Central to positive behaviour management in schools is the recognition that individual self-confidence and self-esteem should be nurtured and maintained. Members of the school community need to be known as individuals and their needs should be met. When problems occur they should be acknowledged and resolved. Success can only be achieved through the identification and meeting of needs. All success, great and small, should be celebrated.

There is much to be celebrated in schools; teachers need to know when they are effective. They also need to know that they can be honest, and that support will be given when it is needed. Managing positive behaviour in schools is a whole-school responsibility based on shared beliefs and values, clear expectations and boundaries, and consistency as reflected in collaborative policies, procedures and practices.

## Useful further reading

*Managing Classroom Behaviour*, D. Fontana (1994). Leicester: BPS Books.

Each chapter provides useful guidance on how to manage behaviour.

*Success Against the Odds*, National Commission on Education (NCE) (1996). London: Routledge.

Each chapter presents an example of how effective management can create a community where positive behaviour is the norm.

*Community Education*, C. Poster (1982). London: Heinemann.

This book illustrates how agencies can work together to serve children and their community.

*Managing Teacher Stress*, W. A. Rogers (1996). London: Pitman.

This is essential reading for all teachers, providing guidance on how to manage themselves and their teams with good effect.

## References

Blandford, S. (1998*) Managing Discipline in Schools*. London: Routledge.

Department for Education (DfE) (1994a) *Code of Practice on the Identification and Assessment of Children with SEN*. London: DfE.

Department for Education (DfE) (1994b) *Pupil Behaviour and Discipline*, Circular 8/94. London: DfE.

Department for Education (DfE) (1994c) *The Education of Children with Emotional and Behavioural Difficulties*, Circular 9/94. London: DfE.

Department for Education (DfE) (1994d) *Exclusions from School*, Circular 10/94. London: DfE.

Department for Education (DfE) (1994e) *The Education by LEAs of Children Otherwise than at School*, Circular 11/94. London: DfE.

Department for Education (DfE) (1994f) *The Education of Sick Children*, Circular 12/94. London: DfE.

Department for Education (DfE) (1994g) *The Education of Children being Looked After by Local Authorities*, Circular 13/94. London: DfE.

Department for Education and Employment (1998) *The Standards Fund* . London: HMSO.

Department of Education and Science (DES) (1989) *Discipline in Schools: Report of the Committee of Enquiry*. London: DES & Welsh Office.

Docking, J.W. (1980) *Control and Discipline in Schools*, London: Harper & Row.

## Education management link resource: Target book

**Target book**

Name: _____

Class: _____

**You**

**Targets**

**Success**

Pupil comment: _____

_____

_____

_____

_____

_____

| Target 1: | |
|---|---|
| To be reached by: | Completed: |

*Chapter 3*

# Organising classrooms to promote learning for all children: two pieces of action research[1]

*Deborah Lucas and Gary Thomas*

As schools become more inclusive there is an argument that children should be included more in our thinking about classroom organisation and design. Children seem to prefer non-traditionally organised classrooms, yet little has been done to find out what *they* think about the ways in which the classroom is organised. This chapter gives the results of two pieces of research about classroom organisation. The first reports on an observation that gives some room for concern about traditional organisation, and the second reports on the results of a major reorganisation of the classroom 'geography'. We conclude that major benefits can come from such reorganisation.

## Children and their environment at school

Vandalism and graffiti are the most conspicuous symptoms of the alienation of children from the built environment generally and schools in particular. While there are many possible causes of this alienation, it is likely that a centrally important one is the absence of a sense of ownership among children for their classrooms and their schools.

If lack of ownership is important, it points to an urgent need to include children in classroom organisation and design. This seems to happen more *outside* schools than within: local authorities now consult children about school and environmental design (Adams and Ingham 1998), although authorities admit to finding such consultation difficult, due, for example, to the absence of the usual consultative channels, such as representative groups. However, where consultation does exist (e.g. Leicester City Council 1992) it rarely includes those 'at the margins': those with disabilities or learning or behaviour difficulties. This is particularly worrying because these children may well be those who feel the greatest degree of alienation.

Perhaps because of the historic neglect of the child's voice, planning has sometimes been guided by stereotypical images of the needs of 'special' or marginal children, images

---

1. Parts of this chapter first appeared in the *British Journal of Special Education* **17**(1), 31–4, and these are reproduced with the kind permission of the editor of that journal.

that involve passivity, vulnerability or weakness (Kitzinger 1990; Rieser and Mason 1990). Recent research (Thomas *et al.* 1998) found that features of school and classroom organisation and design which were assumed by planners to foster access and inclusion were in fact often felt by children, teachers and parents to have been insignificant to the success of inclusion. Although the school environment – from the design of the classroom space to the design of the toilets – ought clearly to be important features for the success of inclusion, it appears that features of design outside those customarily focused on also need to be addressed.

The extent to which schools *enable* inclusion will depend upon children's perception of them, and whether, for instance, they are judged to be attractive, understandable and 'legible'. The obverse of this is that the appearance of environments affects the meanings given to them. If for some children spaces and structures 'speak' difference or disability, this may exaggerate the isolation, devaluation and exclusion of these children (Imrie 1996; Greed and Roberts 1998).

This chapter is premised on two assumptions:

- that the physical organisation of the classroom is important for the kind of learning that occurs therein; and
- that the degree of inclusion which happens will in turn depend on this kind of organisation.

It describes two small-scale research projects in classrooms which examine these assumptions and their effects.

## Research in special education

In special education we have traditionally sought to meet special educational needs through the provision of new or different methods of assessment or teaching, usually to groups of children in settings removed from other children. The problem now, and increasingly, is that in the inclusive settings in which those methods have to be practised there is a host of factors which will conspire against their success. It is increasingly being recognised that inclusion is about more than providing different forms of teaching, but rather about providing good teaching for all. Porter's (1995) comparison of traditional and inclusionary approaches summarises the changes that have taken place in thinking about special needs classrooms in recent years (see Table 3.1).

The thrust of the argument behind the changes summarised in Table 3.1 is that mainstream teachers will find it difficult or impossible to find the time for mastering or using special education's special methods. Neither, it must be said, are these different methods, which special educators have been so good at promulgating, renowned for their success (see, for example, Cashdan *et al.* 1971; Hargreaves 1978; Thomas 1985; Algozzine *et al.* 1986).

The inclusive classroom will depend for its success on changes from within. This demands a complete reappraisal of the methods which have customarily been used to identify and help children who are having difficulties. More flexibility in assumptions about identification; a shift to formulating more effective means of support and team-

**Table 3.1** Porter's (1995) comparison of traditional and inclusionary approaches

| Traditional approach (which may include integration) | Inclusionary approach |
| --- | --- |
| Focus on student | Focus on classroom |
| Assessment of student by specialist | Examine teaching/learning factors |
| Diagnostic/prescriptive outcomes | Collaborative problem-solving |
| Student programme | Strategies for teachers |
| Placement in appropriate programme | Adaptive and supportive regular classroom environment |

work with colleagues (see Thomas 1992), and a willingness to begin considering changes in classroom organisation as ways of meeting children's needs, are all now appropriate. The last of these includes changes in the classroom layout – and this is the focus of the rest of this article.

Not only is it more appropriate now to be thinking of changes in organisation to meet children's needs, but such an approach may also be more productive and simpler than concentrating on individual approaches. Organisational changes do appear to hold out promise and to be made relatively straightforwardly (see DeVault *et al.* 1977; Stallings *et al.* 1986; Wheldall 1988), when compared with the methods that have traditionally been used by special educators.

## Changing classroom geography to meet needs: two pieces of action research

A good way to begin thinking about changing the way the classroom is organised in order to help meet special educational needs is to consider the physical arrangements of the class. The examples which follow aim to illustrate this.

### *Case study 1*

Figure 3.1 shows the results of part of a study made in a classroom of 10- and 11-year-old children. In this classroom the focus was on how often children were 'on-task' (i.e. doing what they were supposed to be doing). Each of the numbers represents an on-task figure.

Two interesting points emerge from this analysis. The first is that those children who are sitting on their own or at the periphery of the classroom activity are, in general, more engaged than those who are in groups. (In fact, those children sitting on their own had moved away from groups – presumably to avoid distraction – by their own choice, and not by teacher direction.)

The second point is that those who are in groups have similar engagement levels. The reason for this became evident when we examined the videotapes on which these figures

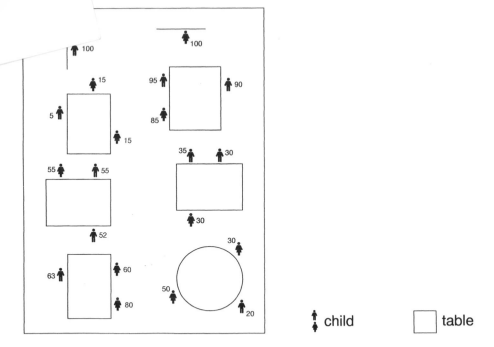

**Figure 3.1**   Children on-task in groups in a classroom of 10- and 11-year-olds

are based. Many of the groups were engaging in the kind of activity which, as teachers, we try to minimise: activities which children usually call 'messing about'.

This leads to the question, *why group?* The answer, of course, lies in the principles which have for many years guided the good child-centred classroom. We want to foster communication, cooperation and imagination, usually through groupwork. But research (see, for example, Tann (1988) for a review) backs up what any experienced observer of the primary classroom knows: children are often asked to do *individual work* in groups.

If this is true, the rationale for grouping evaporates. The very features of groups which make them good for cooperation and communication (e.g. eye-contact with others, the ability to see and talk to a number of other children) make them poor for doing individual work. Children do individual work best in a setting which minimises distraction. They *need* a different kind of classroom set up for it.

Children who are having difficulties are often particularly easily distracted, losing concentration very quickly. These pupils' special needs have to be kept in mind when grouping and other classroom arrangements are being considered, in order that distraction is reduced.

There is, then, scope for thinking about the use of space within the classroom and the best arrangements of that space for helping children who are experiencing difficulty. For instance, instead of putting display tables and cupboards against the wall, teachers might move these out so that they serve the dual function of providing screens and partitions. Easily distracted children may be able to work more consistently at the task in hand if distractions are reduced by this kind of manoeuvre. The next case study illustrates some of these points.

## Case study 2

Among the many systems that I (DL) saw operating in classrooms was one that I felt might be of paramount importance and which I adopted with a class of 26 nine- to ten-year-olds, of mixed abilities and ethnic and social backgrounds in an inner city school. It was classroom layout. Three factors influenced my choice. Firstly, my experience with previous classes, particularly one in an educational priority area, had been that the so-called 'naughty children's table' would at times become a haven of respite for the child overcome by the demands of classroom and home life. Some children would ask to sit there. Secondly, like the teacher before me, I had not taken to the style of teaching children in small groups. Not only did I find children naturally gifted at confounding my carefully planned schedules but I was also sceptical as to the efficacy with which teachers teach and children learn within this system of organisation. It seemed that such seating arrangements did not always enhance the style of learning. Thirdly, I wished to re-integrate a pupil with a statement of special educational needs into her own class. Thus my aims were to match the children's learning, and my teaching, to the classroom geography. As teachers may draw from a range of teaching strategies during their working days the flexibility of any classroom arrangements remains of the utmost importance.

I began reorganising the classroom by removing any furniture I considered superfluous. The children's tables (all two-seaters) were moved out to the walls so that they formed a 'ring' around the perimeter of the room, with their chairs facing outwards towards the walls. I moved the carpet to the centre and positioned four units (one bookcase, two display units and a woodwork bench) at angles on the carpet corners. This was the basic structure of the room. It was very simple and very spacious. The reorganised classroom is shown in Figure 3.2.

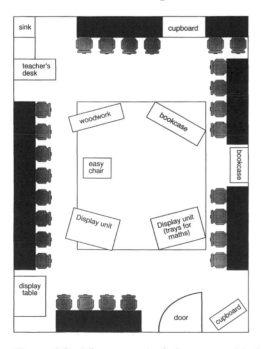

**Figure 3.2**    The reorganised classroom with the children seated round the walls

I set up containers on one display table for the children's work books, leaving their tidy trays available for the maths equipment and, more crucially, promoting the importance of their work. Throughout the year the children were responsible for making covers for all of their exercise books. Thus, the books were personalised and displayed.

On the first day of term I explained why I had done such an odd thing to our new classroom. I told the children that we would use the carpet (the centre of the room) as a meeting place/group work area where we would talk and discuss activities and then move out to the walls to work. Before we left the carpet (or base) we would discuss the nature of the day/session, whether or not it would require moving the tables into groups, who would be talking (in collaborative work) and so on. In this way, an agreement was reached about who was doing what – roles were made explicit. This notion of moving *away* from the centre of the room also produced an air of industry.

One necessary rule came from the children: in sessions devoted to individual work any one child had the right to ask for total silence. I was uncertain about this at the beginning as I did not want to deny purposeful discussion. However, this was the consensus of the class, which perhaps reflected children's perceptions of the workplace. We also decided we would agree on a time to meet back on the carpet to show the work that had been done. This may have motivated some while promoting pride in others. The system was tried for a month and reviewed. As it turned out, the reaction was positive.

During the first week, Susan, a child with a statement of special educational needs, found it hard to adjust to the new system. She had learning and slight coordination diffi-culties and was easily distracted. She had no special place near me, largely because I had no fixed place either. She was part of the circle of children. However, after only a short time, there was a dramatic change in her attitude to herself, her class and her work. She was no longer an outsider but now an insider – part of the circle. During showing times, she would proudly hold up her work and receive encouragement from her classmates. Perhaps it helped them to understand what she was doing and helped her to feel part of the group.

There were other benefits in meeting the children's needs for conditions conducive to individual work and preventing special needs arising.

- There was less possibility for the emergence of a group of children 'setting up camp' on a group table (a familiar occurrence in grouped classrooms). It is much harder to set up camp in a row of tables than a group. Taking this one step further, it is difficult to form hierarchies in a circle.
- It is easier to glance up and see if the teacher is watching you than to have to turn around to do so. The organisation of many classrooms fosters a dependency on the teacher for control, rather than encouraging self-control. With this classroom layout the teacher is no longer the focus – releasing her from 'raised-eyebrow and glare' duty.
- It met the children's needs for a clear, meaningful and workable system.
- Conditions for learning effectively were met. Unless doing group work, most adults would choose to work in conditions of least distraction. Why, then, do we persist in asking children to concentrate when they are seated at groups of tables designed for social interaction? This is not to negate the importance of children's talk in learning,

merely to think more clearly about its role. The noise level in the reorganised classroom was consistently quiet, sometimes disconcertingly so. On reflection, it may simply have been that the new classroom layout had put a spanner in a popular but not invariably ideal system and the children were now given a chance to concentrate.

An interesting spin-off to the new organisation was that playtime became less popular. Motivation had clearly increased.

## Classroom geography and special needs: evidence from other research

In a major review of classroom research, Weinstein (1979) reinforces many of the points made in these case studies. One particularly interesting case study which she cites compared two classrooms which were similar in all but classroom geography.

In classroom A, desks were arranged so that only two or three children could work together. Areas for different activities were set apart by barriers, such as bookcases, and areas for quiet study or activities were also set apart. The teacher's desk was in the corner so that she was unable to direct activities from it and had to move around the room a great deal. In classroom A, conversation was quieter and the children were more engaged, with longer attention spans than in classroom B, where: large groups of children (up to 12) were supposed to be working together (despite the individualised curriculum); areas for different activities were not clearly designated; and the teacher's desk was centrally located – enabling her to direct activity from her seat.

There is evidence that children prefer non-traditionally organised classrooms (i.e. not organised in the traditional Plowden format with groups). Pfluger and Zola (1974), for instance, found that children preferred a large space in the centre of the room, with furniture along the walls. Children may even prefer being in formal rows rather than being in groups (see Wheldall *et al.* 1981; Bennett and Blundell 1983).

Important also for the organisation of the classroom where children with special educational needs are working is the evidence of Delefes and Jackson (1972). They observed that an 'action zone' exists in many classrooms: most of the teacher's interactions occur with children at the front and in the middle of the class (even in classrooms which, in theory, have no front).

Research shows (Saur *et al.* 1984) that, if an action zone exists, hearing impaired children who happen to be sitting at the periphery of the class are doubly disadvantaged. Not only children with sensory disabilities will be handicapped by the action zone: withdrawn children, or the 'intermittent workers' of the ORACLE study (Galton *et al.*, 1980) might also be doubly disadvantaged by the existence of such a zone. There is clearly scope here for thinking about the geography of the classroom, the movement of the teacher around the classroom and the placement of certain children within the class if those children's needs are to be met appropriately.

Linked with the classroom geography are the tasks we are expecting children to do. Johnson *et al.* (1983) have shown that merely putting children into integrated settings and expecting them to get on with it is not enough. Indeed, moving children with special educational needs to ordinary classrooms may have effects very different from those we expected. Johnson *et al.* show that 'special' pupils may be viewed in negative ways whether they are in mainstream classes or not. Physical proximity carries with it the possibility of making things worse rather than better. The success of inclusion schemes seems to depend a lot on how teaching is organised and how interaction among pupils is structured. There is a need, then, also to consider the curriculum and the activities in which children are engaged within the reorganised classroom. It is outside the scope of this article to examine the curricular implications of specific grouping strategies but the reader is referred to Aaronson and Bridgeman (1979), Johnson and Johnson (1986) and Tann (1988) for a fuller discussion of this issue.

## Implications for teaching

Changing the organisation of the classroom is an unfamiliar way of meeting needs, yet is far more in tune with an inclusionary mindset than more traditional methods. It does not necessarily involve the identification of specific children, nor does it require the construction and execution of complex teaching or remedial programmes. By matching organisation with teaching aims, teachers may be able to stop certain difficulties arising and to help children who are experiencing difficulties.

A note of caution should, perhaps, be sounded. Changing the organisation of the classroom, particularly if it is a change which affects other professional colleagues, such as the support teacher, teachers on outreach, specialist teachers (e.g. of hearing impaired children) or classroom assistants ought to involve three key elements: negotiation, planning and evaluation. There are no prescriptions for successful classroom practice; what works for one teacher in one situation may be wrong for another teacher who prefers a different style of teaching and who has different children and different colleagues to work alongside. The only way to establish effective ways of working in the inclusive classroom is through these key processes of negotiation, planning and evaluation.

Nevertheless, the case studies presented here, as well as the reports from the literature, show that significant changes can be made in the way the classroom is organised to cater for special educational needs, and indeed for the needs of all the children in the class. These changes have come about because of small-scale research which has provided powerful insights into the working of the classroom.

## Link resource

Once you have decided on a classroom geography, there is the question of how to organise the work of the children to best effect. Given that children with difficulties or disabilities will often have learning support assistants (LSAs) to help them, it is useful to consider how the work of these additional staff may be organised around the classroom to provide support most effectively. One method which has been shown to work in primary classrooms (e.g. Thomas 1985) is 'room management'. Essentially, this involves the following:

- One person, a teacher or an LSA, takes on the role of an *indiv* concentrating on the work of individual children, working intensively wi... short, specified periods. A programme of children to be worked with is established before the lesson.
- One person – again, teacher or LSA – takes on the role of *activity manager*, working with the rest of the children, and concentrating on their work in groups. This is at a less intensive level, and the activity manager will also take on responsibility for managing the routine and control of the class, dealing with interruptions and other matters.

Using room management, the photocopiable grid on page 36 can be used to help organise the work of the class, including children who may be having difficulties. Having drawn up a lesson plan, you can proceed to specify tasks for four (or more) groups of children in your class, and likely work for individuals who may be experiencing difficulty. (The grid is adapted from Thomas (1985) and Cowne (1996)). You can now draw a rough 'map' of the class specifying the place of the work of groups and individuals, showing on the map the working places of the groups and individuals you have outlined in the grid.

## Conclusions

If all children are to be included in the classrooms of the future, then there is a need to think carefully about how the classroom is organised. Imagination in the way the class-room is organised can pay great dividends for inclusion. If space is at a premium, the changes to classroom layout we describe here can provide benefits not only for children with learning difficulties and disabilities but for all children. The moves we describe involve minimum disruption for the liberation of a great deal of space – simply reorganis-ing most of the groups of tables so that they faced the walls of the classroom instead of operating as tables in the centre is just one example of the kind of simple change which can be made. We have tried to indicate that curricular and social benefits – as well as physi-cal ones – can accrue from changes of this kind.

## Useful further reading

*Excellence for all Children: Meeting Special Educational Needs* (1997). London: DfEE.

The government's 'green paper' giving its ideas on how inclusion should be promoted in schools.

*Primary Special Needs and the National Curriculum*, 2nd edn, A. Lewis (1995). London: Routledge.

This is a comprehensive, thoroughgoing text and is full of practical ideas.

*Maths Links*, available from NASEN Publications, 4–5 Amber Business Village, Amber Close, Tamworth B77 4RP, and *Maths Steps*, available from LDA, Duke St, Wisbech, Cambridge, PE13 2AE.

Ideas for maths and those struggling with it.

*Enhancing Design and Technology in Special Education*, ORT Trust (1995). London: ORT Trust.

Ideas for design and technology. Available from Malcolm Jacobs, ORT Trust, 99 Belmont Avenue, Cockfosters, Herts, EN4 9JS.

*Questions – Exploring Science and Technology KS1–KS3.*

This is a magazine on science and technology produced by the Questions Publishing Company, 27 Frederick St, Hockley, Birmingham, B1 3HH.

*The Good Practice Guide to Special Educational Needs*, P. Widlake (ed.) (1996). Birmingham: Questions Publishing Co.

A treasure chest of practical ideas on special education and the National Curriculum. Good chapters on individual subjects as well as information on assessment and individual education plans (IEPs).

*The Making of the Inclusive School*, G. Thomas, D. Walker and J. Webb (1998). London: Routledge.

The story of how a group of schools managed to include all the children from a neighbouring special school.

# References

Aaronson, E. and Bridgeman, D. (1979) 'Jigsaw groups and the desegregated classroom: in pursuit of common goals', *Personality and Social Psychology Bulletin* **5**(4), 438–46.

Adams, E. and Ingham, S. (1998) *Changing Places: Children's Participation in Environmental Planning.* London: Planning Aid London/The Children's Society.

Algozzine, K. M. *et al.* (1986) 'Classroom ecology in categorical special education classrooms', *Journal of Special Education* **20**(2), 209–17.

Bennett, N. and Blundell, D. (1983) 'Quantity and quality of work in rows and classroom groups', *Educational Psychology* **3**(2), 93–105.

Cashdan, A. *et al.* (1971) 'Children receiving remedial treatment in reading', *Educational Research*, **13**(2), 98–103.

Cowne, E. (1996) *The SENCO Handbook: Working within a Whole-school Approach.* London: David Fulton Publishers.

Delefes, P. and Jackson, B. (1972) 'Teacher pupil interaction as a function of location in the classroom', *Psychology in the Schools* **9**, 119–23.

DeVault, M. L. *et al.* (1977) *Curricula, Personnel Resources and Grouping Strategies.* St. Ann, Mo.: ML-GROUP for Policy Studies in Education, Central Midwestern Regional Lab.

Galton, M. J. *et al.* (1980) *Inside the Primary Classroom.* London: Routledge and Kegan Paul.

Greed, C. and Roberts, M. (eds) (1998) *Introducing Urban Design: Interventions and Responses.* Harlow: Addison Wesley Longman.

Hargreaves, D. H. (1978) 'The proper study of educational psychology', *Association of Educational Psychologists' Journal* **4**(9), 3–8.

Imrie, R. (1996) *Disability and the City: International Perspectives.* London: PCP.

Johnson, D. W. and Johnson, R. T. (1986) 'Mainstreaming and cooperative learning strategies', *Exceptional Children* **52**(6), 553–61.

Johnson, D. W. *et al.* (1983) 'Independence and interpersonal attraction among heterogeneous and homogeneous individuals: a theoretical formulation and a meta-analysis of the research', *Review of Educational Research* **53**(1), 5–54.

Kitzinger, J. (1990) 'Who are you kidding? Children, power and the struggle against sexual abuse', in A. James and A. Prout (eds) *Constructing and Reconstructing Childhood.* London: Falmer.

Leicester City Council (1992) *Policy for Street Play; a Child-friendly Approach to Urban Traffic.* Management: Committee Paper. Leicester: Leicester City Council.

Pfluger, L. W. and Zola, J. M. (1974) 'A room planned by children', in G. J. Coates (ed.) *Alternative Learning Environments.* Stroudsberg, Pa.: Dowden, Hutchinson and Ross.

Porter, G. (1995) 'Organization of schooling: achieving access and quality through inclusion', *Prospects* **25**(2), 299–309.

Rieser, R. and Mason, M. (1990) *Disability Equality in the Classroom: A Human Rights Issue.* London: Inner London Education Authority.

Saur, R. E. *et al.* (1984) 'Action zone theory and the hearing impaired student in the mainstream classroom', *Journal of Classroom Interaction* **19**(2), 21–5.

Stallings, J. *et al.* (1986) 'Effects of instruction based on the Madeline Hunter model on students' achievement: findings from a Follow-Through project', *Elementary School Journal* **86**(5), 571–87.

Tann, S. (1988) 'Grouping and the integrated classroom', in: G. Thomas and A. Feiler (eds) *Planning for Special Needs*, 154–70. Oxford: Blackwell.

Thomas, G. (1985) 'Room management in mainstream education', *Educational Research* **27**(3), 186–93.

Thomas, G. (1992) *Effective Classroom Teamwork: Support or Intrusion?* London: Routledge.

Thomas, G. *et al.* (1998) *The Making of the Inclusive School.* London: Routledge.

Weinstein, C. S. (1979) 'The physical environment of the school: a review of the research', *Review of Educational Research* **49**(4), 577–610.

Wheldall, K. (1988) 'The forgotten A in behaviour analysis: the importance of ecological variables in classroom management with particular reference to seating arrangements', in G. Thomas and A. Feiler (eds) *Planning for Special Needs: A Whole School Approach*, 171–85. Oxford: Basil Blackwell.

Wheldall, K. *et al.* (1981) ' Rows v. tables: an example of the use of behavioural ecology in two classes of eleven-year-old children', *Educational Psychology* **1**(2), 171–84.

Wolfendale, S. (1988) 'Parents in the classroom', in G. Thomas and A. Feiler (eds) *Planning for Special Needs,* 204–27. Oxford: Blackwell.

## Special needs link resource: Planning grid

|  | Group 1 | Group 2 | Group 3 | Group 4 |
|---|---|---|---|---|
| Task, resources, intended learning outcomes |  |  |  |  |
| Role of activity manager |  |  |  |  |
| Role of individual helper |  |  |  |  |

*Chapter 4*

# Catching up with reading: from classroom research to national project

*Diana Bentley and Dee Reid*

This chapter outlines the research that has influenced *The Catch Up Project*, a literacy intervention programme for seven- to eight-year-old struggling readers. That research includes: the study that identified the need for an intervention; the small-scale classroom research project that looked at the most effective use of individual pupil/teacher time with weak readers in Years 2–6; evidence bases for other effective strategies that have been integrated into the Catch Up programme; and the pilot research that first monitored the effectiveness of the programme. The chapter sets the research within the context of how the programme was developed and one of the key assessments from the Catch Up programme, a reading attitude questionnaire, is presented as the link resource.

## Introduction

With the introduction of the National Curriculum in 1988 and the Standard Assessment Tasks at the end of each Key Stage in 1991 many schools, teachers and parents were concerned about the effect on children who had fallen behind with reading. This raised questions about such children's learning needs and how these were being addressed. In a study designed to investigate the levels of support which were currently being offered to children with reading difficulties, Thomas and Davis (1997) canvassed opinions from a national sample of special educational needs coordinators (SENCOs). Questionnaires were returned from approximately 600 schools. This research found that there was no unanimity among SENCOs about whether things had improved or deteriorated since the Education Reform Act 1988 and the Code of Practice (DfE 1994). However, there was clear agreement that children experiencing reading difficulties were given insufficient time with a SENCO and that provision from peripatetic teachers had declined. It was shown that, in addition to those children who were entitled to statutory funding a further 18.4 per cent of children aged eight years had reading difficulties which restricted their access to the National Curriculum. Thomas and Davis concluded that these children were unlikely to catch up with literacy unless they were provided with an intensive but manageable programme at this critical age.

## Developing an intervention programme

Prior to the introduction of guided reading in the Literacy Hour in 1998, most Key Stage 2 teachers endeavoured to set aside extra minutes several times a week to hear children who were struggling with reading. The time was usually spent listening to the child reading, and possibly making a list of any miscues that occurred, but there was rarely enough time to follow this up with questions that ensured the child had read with understanding or to teach the decoding skills that would enable the child to read problem words rapidly.

However research undertaken as early as 1978 questioned whether just 'hearing a child read' for a few minutes a day was as effective as setting aside a longer time on a less frequent basis (see Arnold 1977). With this in mind, we decided to conduct a small-scale investigation to try to find out how teachers might use this individual time most effectively.

We identified three different approaches to working with the individual child in order to establish which was most effective for children who had only made a tentative start with reading. We also decided to integrate research that linked the importance of reading followed by writing (Clay 1980) into each of the three approaches, and to establish the minimum amount of time per week that an adult needed to spend with a child in order to obtain progress.

Twenty children from Years 2–6 who were experiencing reading difficulty were selected from two schools. These children were then randomly allocated to the three approaches. Their progress was measured in terms of their acquisition of a selection from the 100 basic words in *Key Words to Literacy and the Teaching of Reading* (McNally and Murray 1968) and *Word for Word* (Reid 1989).

### *Method 1: Paired reading*

Paired reading was first designed by Roger Morgan (1986) and involves children who find reading difficult and the help of non-professionals. Morgan aimed to devise a programme that was simple to administer and could be used with a wide variety of material. His approach was as follows:

1. Child and tutor select a suitable book.
2. Child and tutor read the text simultaneously and aloud.
3. When the child is sufficiently confident to read a few words or a passage alone, he or she signals this by knocking on the table.
4. The tutor praises this and stops reading, the child continues reading aloud alone until he or she gets stuck on a word.
5. The tutor leaves enough time for the child to try to decode the word but if this does not happen, the tutor supplies the word and then simultaneous reading recommences.

During our research we observed that the advantages of this approach were:

- the child was able to complete more of the book;
- the child was able to read a more challenging (and possibly more interesting text than he or she could manage independently);

- some children liked this as they were less anxious about problem words; and
- it helped with fluency and intonation.

The disadvantages were:

- some children disliked the procedure as it reminded them they could only read with an adult; and
- it disguised the child's cueing strategies.

In conclusion we felt that this approach was most useful with younger children or for carers to use for reading practice at home. In the classroom the approach was only of value if the child read the whole text again, alone, and this was generally felt to be too time consuming.

## Method 2: Self-analysing miscues

In the second approach we asked children to reflect upon how they managed to decode words which caused them some initial problem but which they then self-corrected. In this approach, after the child has self-corrected, the teacher asked the child what he or she had done in order to make the self-correction.

The advantages of this approach were:

- it built upon success and that if children realised how they were achieving word recognition then they would use the same strategies with other problem words;
- it gave children more confidence with cueing strategies; and
- it enabled the teacher to praise the more productive decoding procedures.

The disadvantages were:

- some children did feel threatened by this approach; and
- it could feel interruptive both by the teacher asking the child how he or she decoded the word and by the child self-correcting so often that the meaning of the sentence was lost.

In conclusion this method was felt to be of considerable value to children who were only having few problems with a text i.e. those who were reading at the Standard Assessment Task (SAT) Level 2a or above.

## Method 3: Prepared reading

In this approach the child and the teacher looked through the pictures prior to the child attempting to read the book. The teacher also scanned the text and noted any possible problem vocabulary. Then, when talking about the pictures, the teacher unobtrusively introduced the vocabulary without specifically drawing attention to the words in the text.

We observed the following advantages:

- the teacher was able to stress that the purpose of reading is to understand the text;
- it encouraged reading for meaning because the child already had a grasp of the story;

- problem vocabulary had been introduced in context through the discussion – many children said they were surprised they could 'read' a word when they read the story to the teacher;
- it was very quick to do; and
- it did not disguise the cueing strategies of the child.

The disadvantages were:

- in some cases it was difficult to supply the vocabulary; and
- it did depend on the text having sufficient illustrations to enable the teacher to elicit the story.

This approach proved to be the most effective for the greatest number of children who were performing at the SAT Level 1 or 2c. We therefore decided that prepared reading would be a vital component in an intensive intervention programme as it enabled the child to see that the purpose of reading was to understand the text.

### Other observations from the classroom research

Other general observations during our research also showed quite clearly that the children in all three groups had gained both in confidence and ability beyond that expected by the classroom teachers. Most of the children (16 out of 20) were able to read and write the hundred basic sight words and this enabled them to write with greater ease than at the start of the study. They were assessed as reading at the SAT Level 2a or above. Of the remaining four children, two had left during the course of the study, one boy was still finding great difficulty and was assessed as a level 2c and one girl made such little progress that she was finally awarded a statement. All the children said that they 'quite liked reading' or 'I don't mind reading now' (Bentley and Reid 1995). The knowledge that a ten-minute intervention was enough to make a difference, combined with the observations that the prepared reading approach was most effective, provided a starting point for the next project.

## Developing a national project

In January 1997 the team (Diana Bentley, Suzi Clipson-Boyles and Dee Reid) began to develop the intervention on a larger scale in what was now to be called *The Catch Up Project*. The aim was to develop the programme more fully, disseminate it by means of a training pack and measure its effectiveness more closely. We considered how to formalise our prepared reading approach into a comprehensive programme, which included making more explicit other strategies that had been integrated into the ten-minute teaching time. We also needed to bear in mind the core theories of teaching reading.

### The basics of teaching reading

Although there is still much debate on how to teach reading there is at least general agreement that the main ingredients of such a programme would have to include the following:

- a recognition that the purpose of reading is to understand and respond to the content of the printed word;
- the teaching of strategies to ensure the rapid recognition of words; and
- the teaching of cueing strategies in order to decode unfamiliar words.

## Evidence-based strategies

Our previous survey of existing research to decide what evidence-based approaches could be manageably used as components of an intervention programme was a means of making useful links between theory and practice in order to assist weak readers. Three examples are explained below (other examples of evidence-based strategies can be found in the teacher's manual of the training pack (Bentley *et al.* 2000).

*Linking reading with writing (Clay 1980)*
Clay found that one of the most effective ways to consolidate sight words was to encourage the child to practise spelling those words that they could read within a context but could not read with complete confidence.

*Aims:*
1. to contextualise the teaching of reading and writing within a story text;
2. to help children develop a bank of words that they can recognise quickly and write accurately.

*Catch Up strategy:* After reading, a sentence is selected from the text and used as a focus for writing practice. Words selected are those that have been shown to be uncertain in the initial diagnositic assessments.

*Assisting the child's fluency (Stanovich 1980)*
Stanovich found that fluent readers use processing skills less and are therefore able to pay more attention to meaning and context.

*Aim:* To ensure that the child is reading a text that they can manage fluently.

*Catch Up strategy:* The teacher selects books for each child from a carefully graded list of books to ensure fluent reading. (This also gives the child more confidence and improves self-esteem.) In order to enable children who find reading difficult to experience a rapid and fluent read we also recognised the need for a further teaching session in which a group of children could practise reading with fluency and expression and also provide time for the group to respond to the text . This session requires that the group all read a common text, have the opportunity to respond to guided questions and then to comment constructively upon their own performances.

*Child's attitudes to and perceptions of reading (Medwell 1990)*
In her research into the relationship between children's attitudes to reading and the strategies used when reading, Medwell found that the seven- to eight-year-olds fell into two broad bands: those who had a positive attitude to reading, who saw it as enjoyable, informative, engaging and important; and those who found it difficult and who thought

the whole purpose of reading was to say the words correctly. Those children who had an understanding of the purpose and pleasure of reading made more rapid progress.

*Aim:*    To provide the teacher with information about the child's perceptions of and attitudes towards reading that will help with planning appropriate experiences.

*Catch Up strategy:*    The first of the diagnostic assessments is a reading attitude interview to determine the child's perception of the reading process.

## Consolidating the programme

The programme was consolidated into two sessions per week, plus recommended follow-on games and activities. The two sessions were a ten-minute individual teaching session, teacher and individual child and a 15-minute group reading session.

## The training pack

The completed training pack was launched in January 1998. We aimed to to provide clear, easily readable and manageable reources in order to help classroom teachers to implement the programme. The pack contained:

- a video ( showing the programme in action);
- training notes to accompany the video so that staff could undertake their own school-based INSET;
- a teacher's manual describing the programme;
- a graded booklist (fiction);
- five copies of the pupil progress booklet;
- a photocopiable edition of the pupil progress booklet; and
- a photocopiable book of games and activities which could be used by a classroom assistant or for homework.

Before launching the pack, a pilot version was used in trial schools during the autumn term, 1997. Pupil progress was measured across a ten-week period and teacher responses to the materials were invited via a questionnaire.

## Pilot research

Fifteen schools were selected from Oxfordshire, Berkshire and Milton Keynes. They were chosen to reflect as wide a range as possible using roll size, free school meals, speakers of additional languages and catchment areas (village, town, city). The pupils were selected from Year 3, born between 1 September 1989 and 31 August 1990. They had all achieved a Level 1 for reading in the SATs the previous term. Each school was asked to work with six pupils within this category but some schools were unable to do this, in some cases because they were small schools and had cross-phase classes and in others because of management problems. The mean reading age score for the main Catch Up group ($n = 74$) on the pretest was 6 years 6 months (78.3 months; SD = 6). The average reading age score on the post-test was 7 years (84.4 months: SD = 7.5). The range at this stage was 6 years to 8 years

5 months. This translated to a total reading age increase of 6 months across the ten-week period. In real terms, deducting the ten-week duration, which can be assumed to contribute a time-related maturational increase regardless of intervention, meant an actual gain of 3.5 months.

*The experimental sub-sample*

In order to determine that it was the ingredients of the Catch Up programme that were effective and not just that teachers were spending an equivalent time on an individual and group basis, we also conducted an experimental study to compare different approaches. We selected five Oxfordshire schools to provide a representative cross-section of school types using roll size, free school meals, English as a second language, catchment area and age range as variables. These were carefully matched with two further parallel groups of five shools each.

- The first group of teachers implemented the Catch Up programme, spending ten minutes per week with an individual child and 15 minutes in a group.
- The second group, called the 'matched time' group, was asked to spend the equivalent time but without the Catch Up framework and resources.
- The third group was asked to act as the control group and to proceed with their usual methods of support for these children.

In this experiment the average reading gain for the Catch Up schools was considerably greater than those of both the matched time schools and the control group. The average gain in months was 8.6 for the Catch Up pupils, compared to 3.5 for the matched time group and 1.1 for the control group (see Clipson-Boyles (2000) for further details of the statistics).

Clearly, these early findings needed to be treated with considerable caution due to the small sample size, and indeed other larger studies are currently in progress. However, in the early stages of the project, they provided us with enough encouragement to continue developing the intervention further, and as more and more schools adopt the programme it is becoming increasingly clear that The Catch Up Project is making a considerable positive impact on the needs of struggling readers.

## Implications for teaching

It is clear from our research that unless struggling readers in Year 3 are provided with a planned intervention, they are likely to fall even further behind. However, that intervention needs to be carefully planned with appropriate resources. Schools need to ensure that they have considered the following when undertaking such plans:

- The children should be identified at the end of Year 2 ready to start the intervention at the start of the next term.
- The children should be provided with carefully graded resources which they feel confident to read. It is also important to ensure that the books are new to the child and are at an appropriate interest level in order to remotivate them and coax them back where they may have developed a dislike for reading.

- The intervention should be carefully structured, but also designed to meet the specific needs of each individual child. Focused teaching is more effective than simply hearing them read more often.
- The intervention is particularly effective when the teacher is supported by the head teacher, where the approach is subject to review and where the children's progress is monitored.
- Building positive self-esteem has a positive effect on struggling readers. This involves praising specific strategies, providing manageable tasks and readable texts, and addressing the fact that they may not like reading by taking care to rekindle their interest.

## Link resource

Diagnostic assessments are an important part of the Catch Up programme, and these are provided in the pupil progress booklets. The first assessment is the reading attitude questionnaire. This can provide teachers with an invaluable insight into the child's reading attitudes, habits and perceptions. It also casts light on the reading environment at home. The photocopiable link resource on page 46 will enable you to try this with children in your own class. It is not recommended as a worksheet for children to complete alone, but rather something that teacher and child can share together as a focus for discussion.

## Conclusions

This national project is built upon the work of previous research. Its ongoing development is also inextricably linked with new research: for example the pilot study is now being replicated on a larger scale; the management issues are being examined in a separate study; and the impact of a new CD-ROM resource is also being monitored. What we have tried to do is to link ideas and theories to classroom practice and to observe what works.

A CD-ROM of literacy games in exciting environments was released in spring 1999 to provide additional practice activities for these children (and others like them). An updated edition of the pack was published in January 2000, which now includes the additional non-fiction graded booklist. At the time of writing almost 2000 schools have adopted the Catch Up programme, and the many comments from teachers have been very encouraging, as have been the independent research results from LEAs. The Catch Up programme has been proved to make a marked difference to the progress of struggling readers in Year 3, and although the approach cannot claim to be a guaranteed solution for all children it does offer an effective programme that is grounded in relevant reseach and which is appropriate for use in the busy classrooms of today.

For further details about *The Catch Up Project*, please contact the Project Administrator: Mary Wakefield, School of Education, Oxford Brookes University, Wheatley, OX33 1HX (Tel: 01865 485903); email: catchup@brookes.ac.uk

## Useful further reading

*Supporting Struggling Readers*, D. Bentley and D. Reid (1995). Royston: UKRA Mini Books.

This booklet describes in more detail the research looking at the different ways of hearing children read and suggests practical ways to help struggling readers.

*Locating and Correcting Reading Difficulties*, E. Ekwall and J. Shanker (1992). London: Macmillan.

Each chapter covers a range of topics (for example decoding abilities, comprehension abilities, study skills abilities) and contains useful lists of assessment records.

*Helping Children with Reading and Spelling*, R. Reason and R. Boote (1994). London: Routledge.

This book offers a basic list of suggestions to help children who struggle with learning to read and spell. It contains much useful photocopiable material and case examples.

*Paired Reading, Spelling and Writing*, K. Topping (1995). London: Cassell.

This book describes specific structured methods for developing and improving children's reading ability. There is detailed advice about successful organisation and many valuable photocopy masters.

## References

Arnold, H. (1977) *Listening to Children Reading*. London: Hodder and Stoughton.

Bentley, D. and Reid, D. (1995) *Supporting Struggling Readers*. Royston: UKRA.

Bentley, D. *et al.* (2000) *The Catch Up Programme,* updated edition. Oxford: Oxford Brookes University.

Clay, M. (1980) 'Early writing and reading: reciprocal gains', in Clark, M. and Glynn, T. (eds) *Reading and Writing for the Child with Difficulties*, 27–43. Edgbaston: University of Birmingham.

Clipson-Boyles, S. (2000) 'The Catch Up Project: a reading intervention in Year 3 for Level 1 readers', *The Journal of Research in Reading* **23**(1), 78–84.

Department for Education (1994) *Code of Practice on the Identification and Assessment of Special Needs*. London: HMSO.

McNally, J. and Murray, W. (1968) *Key Words to Literacy and the Teaching of Reading*. London: Schoolmaster Publishing Company.

Medwell, J. (1990) 'What do children think about reading – does it matter?', in Harrison, C. and Ashworth, E. (eds) *Celebrating Literacy, Defending Literacy*, 104–14. Oxford: Blackwell.

Morgan, R. (1986) *Helping Children Read*. London: Methuen.

Reid, D. (1989) *Word For Word*. Wisbech: Learning Development Aids.

Stanovich, K. (1980) 'Towards an interactive compensatory model of differences in the development of reading fluency', *Reading Research* **16**(1), 32–71.

Thomas, G. and Davis, P. (1997) 'Special needs: objective reality or personal construction? Judging reading difficulty after the code', *Educational Research* **39**(3), 263–70.

Topping, K. (1995) *Paired Reading, Spelling and Writing*. London: Cassell.

## English link resource: Reading attitude questionnaire

**Reading attitude questionnaire**

Name: _____

Class: _____


What is the best story you have ever read? _____

Do you like reading to your teacher? _____

Do you like reading at home? _____

Do you have any books of your own at home? _____

Does anyone at home read to you? _____

Do you like stories or information books? _____

_____

_____

_____

_____

What do you think reading is? _____

_____

_____

_____

_____

What do you do when you read? _____

_____

_____

_____

_____

If you knew someone who couldn't read, what would you tell them to do? _____

_____

_____

_____

_____

*Chapter 5*

# Reading and writing arithmetic

*Alison Price*

This chapter examines how teachers can help children to record their mathematics and make sense of the recordings of others. It will consider the implications of theoretical research into the nature of mathematics learning, of research into children's understanding of mathematics in and out of the classroom, of my own study into a developmental approach to teaching and learning early mathematics, and current research into the teaching and learning of early addition. It will look at alternative ways to introduce children to mathematical recording and finally develop these ideas to look at how the use of writing frames, encouraged in the National Literacy Strategy, can be used by older children to explain and record their mathematics.

## Introduction

There is a key sense in which mathematics is a cerebral activity, carried out in the head. Yet most adults, including many primary teachers, see the essential element of mathematics as being bound up in the signs and symbols used to record it. The relationship between symbols and meanings in mathematics is less clear than it is with written words. The relationship between spoken and written language has some direct correspondence as, once the key elements of sound and symbols (e.g. f . . . ee . . . d) have been mastered, it is possible to attempt the reading of new words and gain understanding of their meaning from the context of the text. Children can soon move on from concentration on the sounds and forms of letters to concentration on what the text is saying, or to what they want to express in their own writing.

   However, in the teaching of mathematics, numerals (1, 2, 3 . . .) and other mathematical signs (e.g. +, =, > . . .) consist of a much more concentrated meaning, which can neither be inferred from the context nor pronounced without prior knowledge. For example, the subtraction sign can be used to record 'take away', 'the difference between', 'subtract', or 'minus'. Sometimes the sign represents a single word and sometimes a phrase. Sometimes it represents spoken language, which would be said in the same order as it is written:

e.g.        $6 - 5 = 1$

        six take away five equals one

but sometimes it may be said in a different order

        the difference between six and five is one.

Traditionally, children have not been taught to use these symbols to communicate meaning in mathematics. They see symbols on the page not as a form of communication, as an indication of the relationship between numbers within the number system, but only as an instruction to do something.

## What are symbols?

Symbols are essentially a form of culturally defined tool. In mathematics they serve two purposes. First they enable us to manipulate and to calculate with large numbers, as well as to record what we have done. Just try to imagine multiplying three hundred and forty-six by seven hundred and fifty-nine in your head, or on paper or with a calculator, without recourse to numerals. Unless you have a very strong image for number, a mental image of an abacus for example, then you probably cannot do it. So mathematical symbols are essential to more complex arithmetic skills. But there is a second purpose for mathematical symbols; that of recording and communicating mathematics. Young children learning mathematics must understand the use of symbols in recording.

### Symbols, signs and numerals

Much of the literature on symbols is unclear about the difference in meaning between the words sign and symbol. In fact, the dictionary gives each as part of the definition of the other. I find it helpful to use symbol to refer to any written mark used to record mathematics. Symbols can then be subdivided into:

- numerals – symbols which denote number or quantity (7, 2·5, ½, etc.); and
- signs, which indicate the relationships between numbers ( +, –, =, >, etc.).

## Making connections

One of the ways of looking at how children learn mathematics is based on the work of Jerome Bruner (1967), who developed a framework for concept learning. He proposed that the concept can be seen to consist in 'enactive' form (carrying out operations using practical equipment), 'iconic' form (mental or actual representations of what is done in pictorial or diagrammatic form) and 'symbolic' form (representation in words and symbols). This idea has been adapted by various mathematics educators including Liebeck (1984) and Haylock and Cockburn (1997). Their models differ in the emphasis they give to teaching and learning, but they all claim that in order to have a clear understanding of the concept, children must be able to make connections between what they do, what they say and how this is recorded on the page. For example, the Haylock and Cockburn connections model indicates that in order to understand a concept in mathematics the learner must be able to move from any one representation of that concept to any other. This is shown in Figure 5.1.

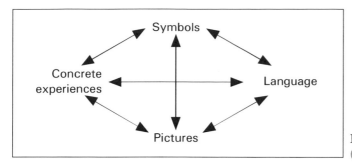

**Figure 5.1** Connections model (after Haylock and Cockburn 1997)

So, symbols can be seen as just one way of representing the concept, which children need to be able to relate to all other representations. Can we therefore relate how children learn to use mathematical symbols with how they learn to read and write?

### Writing mathematics

Learning to read and write consists of several elements which eventually come together for the child. Children encounter written text in books and the environment. This text is read to them by others, but at first there is no expectation that they will be able to read it for themselves. Meanwhile, the children are developing their understanding of spoken language, refining their ability to communicate orally. As they grow older they begin to recognise words for themselves, and the teaching of phonics further enables the development of decoding skills to read previously unseen words. At the same time, children begin to make their own marks on paper, which they interpret as writing. Training in handwriting, in reading, in spelling and oral communication come together as the children become more efficient writers. This development, which concentrates on celebrating the child's developing skills while bringing them closer to the socially accepted norm of writing, has been termed developmental or emergent writing.[1]

The same is rarely true of learning to write mathematics. Here the demand for formal recording of symbols has traditionally been introduced *at the same time* as the words and concepts they represent. The children are asked to understand, to talk about, to read and to write mathematical concepts simultaneously, or at least within a very short period of time. This is less of a problem for older children and adults who are confident about how to record their ideas and have already learnt how to use a system of symbols, but for primary school children we may be asking too much. You may be able to think back to your own introduction to algebra with its new notation system to remind yourself just how confusing symbols without understanding can be.

So children are being introduced to formal symbols through the written page rather than learning to write it for themselves. They are being taught to read mathematics but not to write it. The most the children do is to 'fill in the answer' at the end of the sentence.

---

1. Although some writers use the term emergent, I prefer to use developmental since it indicates that the child continues to develop, rather than there being a discontinuity between emerging and more formal writing.

It is as if they were being taught to write through cloze procedure activities and never expected to express ideas for themselves. This results in the understanding that an arithmetic equation or number sentence is an instruction rather than conveying information about the relationships between numerical quantities.

The emphasis on oral and mental arithmetic in the National Numeracy Strategy (DfEE 1999) is partly designed to overcome this. In accordance with the strategy, children are encouraged to learn about the concepts and talk about them, to become proficient with the ideas, before being expected to work with them on paper. But the strategy does not clearly address how teachers should introduce formal notation to the children. What can we learn from research about this process?

## Research on children using mathematical symbols

A key work in the area of children's understanding of symbols is that by Martin Hughes (1986). In his 'tins game', Hughes asked children to record on the top of each tin the number of bricks that had been hidden inside. He found that most of the children were able record something which they could read back as the correct number, with the older children using recognisable numerals to do so. However, when he asked them to record a change in the number of bricks, either the addition or removal of a small number of them, *none of the children* used formal addition, subtraction or equals signs to record the operation, despite the fact that these children were already doing formal 'sums' in their mathematics lessons in class. He concluded that the children did not understand the communicative function of these signs.

Penny Munn (1998) found that successful use of symbols in school mathematics was predetermined by the child's ability to use some way of recording number in the preschool years, but not necessarily the use of conventional numerals. A child who was able to write numbers but not understand their use had less understanding than a child who could invent symbols and use them meaningfully.

Many of the errors children make in their mathematics arise from a poor understanding of written symbols and the separation of this understanding from mathematics in the real world (e.g., see Cockburn 1999). Richard Skemp blamed the early introduction of formal symbols claiming that 'in the all-important early years, we should stay with spoken language much longer. The connections between thought and spoken words are initially much stronger than those between thoughts and written words, or thoughts and mathematical symbols' (Skemp 1989: 103). Constance Kamii (Kamii and DeClark 1985) questions the early introduction of formal conventions of place value. This results in the introduction of formal algorithms, procedures for setting out and solving calculations such as hundreds, tens and units column subtraction or long division, with the result that children concentrate on the form of the calculation rather than the meaning behind it.

Terezinha Nunes and her colleagues in Brazil (Nunes Carraher 1991) investigated the mathematics used by the street children of Brazil. These children successfully sold goods on the street corners and market stalls, yet did badly in school mathematics. They found that the children (aged 9 to 13 years) solved 98 per cent of the mathematics correctly at the market, 74 per cent when given the same calculations to do as a word problem but only 37 per cent when given it as computational exercises (number sentences). The children were unable to relate their informal, effective calculations to the symbols on the page and instead would try to solve these by remembering how to do the school-taught procedures, generally without success.

## Developing a developmental approach

My own research into this area was the basis for my Masters dissertation (Price 1993). As a practising infant teacher I was concerned that there seemed a mismatch between the way that I taught English through a developmental approach and the way that I taught mathematics, where the children were required to jump through hoops of my making, learning the same things in the same order as one another and recording it formally from the start.

Through action research I tried to apply the principles of developmental writing to my mathematics teaching and evaluated the results. This was a small-scale project which looked at my own teaching and the learning of the 29 children in my class (Years 1 and 2). I found that it was possible to encourage children to record their mathematics in an informal way to start with, and negotiate increasing formalisation of this, with the result that the children showed a greater understanding of the meaning and use of mathematical symbols.

At the start of the year the children were given a mathematics notebook containing plain pages in which they recorded their mathematics. Much of the mathematics was practical, carried out through cooperative group work and games. During, or at the end of, each mathematics lesson the children were encouraged to write or draw something to remind them what they had been doing. Later I also explained that their parents would be coming in for parents evening and would want to see what they had been doing in mathematics, giving them increased purpose for communicating mathematics clearly. To begin with their recordings would often have little mathematical content. They might draw a picture of a group of children around the table, or a collection of bricks. I would discuss with them what the picture showed and how it related to what they had learnt mathematically. Gradually they learnt to emphasise the mathematics rather than the context in their recording. As their writing skills developed they would also use written words to help explain what they had done.

While allowing the children to record in their own way, I also modelled the recording process with them when doing mental arithmetic on the carpet. I tried to use more mathematical symbols in the classroom. The use of numerals in the environment can be developed in classroom activities and display. The contexts of money, bus and telephone numbers, instructions for the number of people allowed to play in the sand tray, etc., give ample opportunity for the use of numerals. Displays can easily be labelled with numerals and a home-made number track from 1 to 145 (we ran out of wall) emphasised ordinal number. I found it more difficult to find real world examples of written calculations. Those that I did use often resulted from class stories or songs which could be explained in mathematical terms. Over the year the children began to use formal symbols for themselves.

My current qualitative, ethnographic research into the learning of addition has involved observation of children's learning over time. I have noted that, for the Reception class children I observed (4–5-year-olds), it was at least ten weeks after the introduction of the addition symbol (+) before the children could start to use it appropriately unaided. Many of the children, especially the youngest in the class, took longer than this. They all found recording using numerals easier than the use of relationship signs (Price 1999).

### Negotiating meaning in the classroom

Work by other researchers and in other countries has also shown that allowing the children to record informally and to discuss and negotiate meaning can encourage both understanding of the mathematics and understanding of its recording.

Realistic Mathematics Education is a movement in The Netherlands which starts from the premise that mathematics was invented to solve problems and this is how children should reinvent it for themselves (Streefland 1991). However, this is not seen as an individual but as a social activity. Gravemeijer defines it as 'an approach for mediating between concrete and abstract based on self-developed models. We may characterise this as "bottom-up" since the initiative is with the students' (Gravemeijer 1997: 316). This is in contrast with teaching practices where the mathematical methods begin with the teacher and children must learn to reproduce them. Children are given problems to solve, then their answers are discussed by the whole class to identify the different methods which can be used to solve the problem and the different ways these can be recorded. The children are encouraged to discuss their results and refine their methods over time.

Similarly, work in the USA by Paul Cobb, Erna Yackel and Terry Wood (Cobb *et al.* 1991; Cobb 1994) shows how through discussion and negotiation, meaning for mathematics and mathematical symbolic recording can be developed in the elementary school. Teaching in this way requires a self-reliant, problem-solving, conjecturing atmosphere where all the participants can interact with trust and empathy.

## Implications for teaching

### Introducing children to symbols

If we accept that children need to be introduced to mathematical symbols in a similar way to their introduction to the written word then we must identify what they must do in the classroom to develop their recording. From the research described in this chapter I would conclude that they need the following:

- They must learn about mathematics through practical and situated activities and through spoken language so that they can articulate the mathematics that they will eventually be asked to record. At every level of new mathematics learning they need to be able to speak mathematics before they are expected to read and write it.
- They must see the mathematical symbols in use. Mathematical symbols must be around in the classroom environment. When teaching children to calculate mentally in the early years of schooling, teachers need to model how the spoken language can

be recorded. The children should not be expected to record formally for themselves at this stage. As they become familiar with the symbols they can be encouraged to read them together with the teacher.

- They must understand the need to record their mathematics as a means of communication. They should be given opportunities to make their own recordings. One way to do this would be to ask them to record what they had been doing in order to share it with the rest of the class in the plenary session at the end of lesson. The children will need feedback on this. The teacher's role is to explain and encourage the positive aspects of that communication, e.g.:

'I like the way you have drawn (. . .) so we all know what you did.'
'How can we tell if you added or subtracted these numbers?'
'How do we know which of these is the answer?'
'What could we write here to make it clearer?'

- Finally the children may need help in forming the symbols, especially some of the more complex numeral shapes. I would recommend that this is seen in the context of handwriting practice rather than mathematics lessons since it is essentially a handwriting skill. Children having difficulty forming the numerals, perhaps because of poorly developed fine motor skills, should not see themselves as being poor at mathematics as a result.

The combination of understanding the need to record mathematics, familiarity with symbols used by the teacher and in the classroom environment, ability to write the symbols, understanding of the mathematical concept, and ability to explain this orally, will then come together in the increasing meaningful use of formal symbols.

## *Developing mathematical communication through the use of writing frames*

Once children understand the need for recording mathematics, and are able to do so using formal mathematical symbols, they will move on to the manipulation of these symbols to calculate with larger numbers. More research needs to be carried out into the way that teachers can help children to move from informal to more formal recording of more complex arithmetic, especially if society continues to see the formal algorithms (e.g. long multiplication and division) as an endpoint for calculation in primary mathematics. As I write, the training of teachers in this aspect of the National Numeracy Strategy is proving controversial. However, children will also need to develop their ability to communicate mathematics. One of the ways that this can be developed is through the use of mathematical writing frames.

As a result of research by the Exeter Extending Literacy Project (EXEL), Maureen Lewis and David Wray developed the concept of writing frames to support children's writing. The frame provides 'a skeleton outline to scaffold children's non-fiction writing . . . [and] gives children a structure within which they can concentrate on communicating what they want to say' (Lewis and Wray 1998: 1). Writing frames have subsequently been adopted by the National Literacy Strategy. Their use is recommended not only for writing in literacy lessons but for structuring writing across the curriculum. What might a mathematics writing frame look like?

## Developing a mathematical writing frame

Here I want to show how a writing frame has been developed to record a particular mathematical problem-solving activity. By taking you through the process I hope that you will not only be able to understand how it can be used with children in this context, but also know how to construct your own frames for different contexts. A photocopiable example of the frame is provided on page 58.

We start by identifying the question.

---

**The problem is...**

e.g.  we want to sell orange drinks at the summer fete. One bottle of squash costs £1.04. How much should we charge to make a 50% profit?

---

With most problems of this sort it is a good idea to identify what we already know and what we need to find out. This encourages the children to think about the question rather than just jumping into symbol manipulation. It identifies the structure for our next two frames.

---

**I already know...**

e.g.  the cost of a bottle of squash and the profit margin.

---

**I need to find out...**

e.g.  how many glasses we can make from one bottle of squash.
      I can then work out how much to charge.

---

I wanted to add a subsidiary question here. When dealing with real-life contexts there are often issues which would be relevant to a real situation but may not be worth including in a mathematics exercise. It is good to encourage the children to consider these even if they are not acted upon.

---

**I also need to consider...**

e.g.  how many we want to make. If we buy too many and don't sell them then we may not make a profit. Should we charge extra to pay for the paper cups, the time people spend making and selling the orange drinks, the cost of washing up if we use proper cups? *(You may want to ignore these but should be aware that they would influence your results.)*

---

Having identified what is the necessary information and finding that out, there needs to be space to record the necessary calculations, although these may be solved using a calculator rather than by pencil and paper.

---

**Calculations**

e.g.  We tested how strong people like their orange and found we needed 25 millilitres per cup. The bottle holds 1 litre so we can make

$$1000 \div 25 = 40 \text{ cups per bottle}$$

Paper cups cost 3p each, so we would pay 120p for 40 cups.
The total cost for 40 drinks is

| Orange | 104p |
|--------|------|
| Cups   | + 120p |
|        | 224p |

Cost per drink is then $224 \div 40 = 5.6p$
50% profit is half as much again.
I'm going to call the cost per drink 6p. so half is 3p. We should charge
$6p + 3p = 9p$ altogether to make a 50% profit.

---

It is then necessary to direct attention back to solving the original question. This includes encouraging the children to interpret the results in the light of the context. Mathematics is not just about calculations. It is a tool to help us to solve real-world problems but it cannot tell us what action to take. It will always need interpretation.

---

**I have found out that...**

e.g.  we will have to charge 9p per cup.
If we sell 100 cups of orange we will make about £3 profit.
This does not seem very much.

---

## Conclusions

Mathematical symbols are part of the way people communicate their ideas. Children need to be taught to communicate in mathematical symbols just as they need to be taught to communicate in written language. Research has shown us some of the problems children have in understanding and using symbols and some of the reasons for these. I have suggested ways that children can learn to record their mathematics in the classroom, how this can be introduced to young children and how it can be developed as the children's mathematical understanding develops.

I believe that if we can teach children that recorded mathematics is a form of communication, mathematics itself will become a more natural and less esoteric activity. The children will not just be doing mathematics but also see mathematics as a form of communication.

## Useful further reading

*Mathematics With Reason*, S. Atkinson (ed.) (1992). London: Hodder and Stoughton.

This book addresses early mathematics from an 'emergent' perspective – an enjoyable read with lots of practical ideas for the classroom.

*Children and Number*, M. Hughes (1986). Oxford: Blackwell.

This is a key work on young children's understanding of arithmetic and recording, accessible for the teacher.

*Problems of Representation in the Teaching and Learning of Mathematics*, C. Javier (ed.) (1987). Hillsdale, NJ: Lawrence Erlbaum.

A collection of more academic papers show the ways that mathematics are represented in the classroom.

*Writing Across the Curriculum: Frames to Support Learning*, M. Lewis and D. Wray (1998). Reading: Reading and Language Information Centre.

This book discusses the ways that writing frames can be used across the curriculum including mathematics.

*Symbols and Meaning in School Mathematics*, D. Pimm (1995). London: Routledge.

This book provides a more theoretical discussion of the relationship between language and symbols in mathematics.

## References

Bruner, J. S. (1967) *Toward a Theory of Instruction*. Cambridge, Mass.: Belknap Press.

Cobb, P. (ed.) (1994) *Learning Mathematics: Constructivist and Interactionist Theories of Mathematical Development*. Dortrecht: Kluwer.

Cobb, P. *et al.* (1991) 'A constructivist approach to second grade mathematics', in von Glasersfeld, E. (ed.) *Radical Constructivism in Mathematics Education*. Dortrecht: Kluwer.

Cockburn, A. (1999) *Teaching Mathematics With Insight*. London: Falmer Press.

Department for Education and Employment (DfEE) (1999) *National Numeracy Strategy: Framework for Teaching Mathematics*. London: DfEE.

Gravemeijer, K. (1997) 'Mediating between concrete and abstract', in Nunes, T. and Bryant, P. (eds) *Learning and Teaching Mathematics*, 315–45. Hove: Psychology Press.

Haylock, D. and Cockburn, A. (1997) *Understanding Mathematics in the Lower Primary Years*. London: PCP.

Hughes, M. (1986) *Children and Number*. Oxford: Blackwell.

Kamii, C. and DeClark , G. (1985) *Young Children Reinvent Arithmetic*. New York: Teachers College Press.

Lewis, M. and Wray, D. (1998) *Writing Across the Curriculum: Frames to Support Learning*. Reading: Reading and Language Information Centre.

Liebeck, P. (1984) *How Children Learn Mathematics*. London: Penguin.

Munn, P. (1998) 'Symbolic function in pre-schoolers', in Donlan, C. (ed.) *The Development of Mathematical Skills*, 47–71. Hove: Psychology Press.

Nunes Carraher, T. (1991) 'Mathematics in the street and in schools', in Light, P. *et al.* (eds) *Learning to Think*, 223–35. London: Routledge.

Price, A. J. (1993) *Developing a Concept of Number at Key Stage One: Can the Principles of Developmental Writing Help?* Unpublished MA (Ed) Dissertation, Open University.

Price, A. J. (1999) *What is the Relationship Between the Teaching and Learning of Early Addition in the Primary Classroom?* 23rd International Conference for the Psychology of Mathematics Education, Haifa, Israel: Technion (published on the Internet at www.fmd.uni-osnabrueck.de/ebooks/erme/cerme1-proceedings/cerme1_contents1.html).

Skemp, R. R. (1989) *Mathematics in the Primary School*. London: Routledge.

Streefland, L. (ed.) (1991) *Realistic Mathematics Education in the Primary School*. Utrecht: Freudenthal Institute.

**Mathematics link resource: Mathematics writing frame**

The problem is:

I already know:

I need to find out:

I may need to consider:

Calculations:

I have found out that:

# Chapter 6

# Science: the need for an environmental focus

*David Mancey*

This chapter describes some of the findings derived from studies on children's ideas and understandings about the natural environment, and explores how these could be used to promote effective science teaching within the primary school. Approaches to applying these within the new science curriculum and the wider curriculum for primary education are provided and a photocopiable discussion framework is provided as a link resource.

## Introduction

In recent years there has been a growing number of research studies to show that children of all ages are generally more informed about issues in the natural environment, such as air pollution and the threat to species through habitat destruction, than children in previous decades. This is likely to have resulted from more media interest in the environment and the feelings of many primary teachers that children want to know more about the real world. Despite this, linking science teaching to issues in the environment has not been a strong feature of the National Curriculum between 1988 and 1999; the new National Curriculum from 2000, as we shall see later, attempts to redress this. The three research studies referred to in this chapter indicate that children often hold inadequate scientific ideas which fail to support their understanding of environmental issues beyond a fairly superficial level.

The structure of the National Curriculum sends a message to teachers that science should be taught in a discrete way in order to achieve the criteria within the programmes of study. It is clear that the level of understanding required from children at the ages of 7 and 11 with respect to science in the natural environment is not very high. Statements such as ' different plants and animals are found in different habitats' (DfE 1995: 46) have a somewhat limited value as they stand, since they are not intended to embrace wider issues that are evident all around us. Arguably, this implies that children are not yet ready to take on board the bigger issues. Likewise, the Qualifications and Curriculum Authority (QCA) science schemes of work (DfEE 1998), now used by many schools, reinforce the notion that science should be detached from issues in the real world. The worry is that teachers may think they *are* making the connections because of the titles of the QCA sections (e.g. 'habitats' and 'interdependence and adaptation'). Some provision for exploring environmental issues can be found in the National Curriculum for geography, although no clear connections are made to the science curriculum. The new geography curriculum is a 'slimmer' version of the previous one; the concern is that as government puts greater emphasis, and hence curriculum time, on literacy and numeracy, there will insufficient space to teach the environmental aspects of geography in primary schools in the future. There is also a lost opportunity for using literacy to develop environmental ideas.

An alternative approach to teaching science discretely is to teach parts of it in a more holistic way, with a greater emphasis on using enquiry-based methods and with the opportunity to provide an environmental context for learning. Some education programmes within Europe, including those in Germany, The Netherlands and Scotland (SOED 1993) already do this. Such approaches could embrace environmental issues without losing sight of what good primary science is all about. On the contrary, the motivation derived from this more applied approach would both encourage development of children's scientific skills and concepts and further their understanding of environmental issues. It would also allow some dovetailing of geography and science, for mutual benefit. What I am suggesting is a range of holistic scenarios coupled with an 'in depth' probing of specific examples that are relevant to primary children. In their report *Beyond 2000*, Millar and Osborne (1998) saw the need to release the science curriculum from an overburden of content by moving to notions of 'explanatory stories'; overviews for our current understandings of science ideas are a key part of this thinking. As an example, 30 years ago there was little debate in scientific circles about the effects of water pollution on life, but now this is not only a societal issue but a statutory part of the primary national curriculum.

## Environmental science research

Three specific research studies are used here to support the argument for this holistic approach to primary science. The first is a Market and Opinion Research Institute (MORI) survey (MORI 1993) into the insights and ideas revealed by 1000 children between the ages of 8 and 15 years. Children were asked to respond to ten carefully selected questions, which probed their concerns about global environmental problems and local environmental problems. From this survey the highest levels of response (>75 per cent) were as follows:

| | |
|---|---|
| cutting down tropical forests | (90%) |
| polluting the oceans | (90%) |
| damaging the ozone layer | (86%) |
| animal extinctions | (86%) |
| inadequate food for humans | (84%) |
| litter | (80%) |
| air pollution from traffic | (78%) |

Overall, the children in this study showed a high awareness of some of the major environmental issues in the local and global environment. Interestingly, global warming (71 per cent) and drinking water supplies (21 per cent) were not identified as such major concerns in this survey. Farming was not mentioned at all, despite being highly relevant to overall use of the environment. Children also showed an overall willingness to be active in environmental action. The highest responses were as follows:

| | |
|---|---|
| recycling cans, bottles and paper | (75%) |
| planting trees | (65%) |
| creating safe areas for wildlife | (63%) |
| not wasting electricity and water | (59%) |

The MORI researchers concluded that children had a high level of interest in the environment and that more could be done to increase children's involvement at a practical level. This study did not intend to probe the scientific concepts held by children. However, this was explored in the next study described below.

The second research project was a set of studies carried out in the University of Leeds as an extension to the Children's Learning in Science (CLIS) research programme, from 1990 to 1996. The papers focused specifically on children's ecological understandings between the ages of 5 and 16 years. The findings for the 5–11 age range are described here. The researchers used a mixture of paper and pencil and interview methods to explore understandings in about 200 children across the whole age range. The responses relevant to this chapter are:

- an increasing recognition of the role of plants in populations;
- a low level of understanding on consequences of ecosystem disruption;
- a generally good understanding of the needs of plants to grow;
- a low level of response on how plants obtain materials(e.g. minerals) to produce food; and
- an increasing understanding of the role of organisms in the decay process.

These findings indicate a need for far more targeted teaching to help primary children make sense of the science within environmental issues. Their awareness of the environment, gained from the media and from their everyday experience, does not appear to provide them with a sufficiently deep understanding of the underlying scientific concepts involved.

The third small-scale research study is one that was conducted on a group of Year 5/6 children in an Oxfordshire primary school during 1996 (Mancey 1996), and reaffirmed the findings of the previous two studies. Ten children were chosen to reflect both gender and ability within the cohort. The method used was to interview children individually and ask them to give explanations to visual materials relating to particular concepts in environmental science. The stimuli and questions are shown in Table 6.1.

The responses were subsequently analysed for language connections to the key concepts. As mentioned earlier, the Key Stages 1/2 science programmes of study up to 1999 made some reference to all these ideas, but without the emphasis provided by this type of questioning. The findings from this research, for children towards the end of their primary education, revealed:

**Table 6.1**    Stimuli and questions used in the Mancey (1996) study

| Stimulus | Question |
| --- | --- |
| Photo of a flower-rich meadow<br>*Concept:* species diversity | Why do you think some fields do not have so many flowers in them? |
| Photo of an oak woodland<br>*Concept:* food web | This is an oak woodland. If the trees were to die, can you say what else might die? |
| Photo of children with nets at a pond<br>*Concept:* species diversity | This pond may have small animals in it. How many types might the children find? |
| Photo of foamy polluted river<br>*Concept:* effects of pollution | This is a river where not many animals are living. Can you suggest reasons for animals not living here? |
| Photo of tropical rain forest<br>*Concept:* key environmental factors | This is a photo of a tropical rain forest. This forest contains more animals than forests in this country. Can you suggest why? |
| Photo of Oxford Botanic Garden<br>*Concept:* conservation | This shows a botanic garden full of different plants from different countries. Why might such gardens be good for plants? |

- a poor understanding of the reasons for loss of biodiversity – several children attributed loss of biodiversity to the weather;
- a poor understanding of the role of trees in food webs – none of the children mentioned that plants make food, and several talked about the loss of oxygen if trees were removed;
- a good knowledge of a variety of animal life in ponds – a high proportion of invertebrates were mentioned in this sample;
- a variable understanding of the effects of pollution – some children could specify types of pollution, others were very superficial; and
- a poor understanding of conservation of genetic resources – most children viewed botanic gardens as gardens, a minority recognising their genetic value.

The results from these studies imply that there is scope for further science understandings. Linking to a wider educational and environmental contexts could facilitate the learning process.

## Implications for teaching

Earlier in this chapter I referred to the way that both the previous science National Curriculum and the revision for 2000 see the importance of children gaining increasing understanding of scientific concepts, increasingly using the natural environment as a context for learning. Implicit in this model is the notion that younger children are 'not ready' to take on board the bigger issues in environmental science. With many primary schools now using some or all of the QCA science schemes of work the concern is that we adopt a more stereotyped and possibly less motivating approach to science, particularly environmental science, in primary schools. By adding 'sustainable development' and 'environmental education' into Key Stages 1 and 2, the government has implied that primary schools could, and *should*, be doing much more to provide a relevant education for the children of the next century.

## What are the educational issues?

- It must be recognised that the science National Curriculum is the *minimum* entitlement that children should receive in schools.
- There is no statutory requirement for science to be taught in a particular way, nor any prescription as to the teaching and learning methods teachers might use for effective teaching. QCA-type schemes were not meant to be prescriptive.
- Teachers need to have sufficient training to be confident in their knowledge of environmental science. Previous research on primary teachers' scientific knowledge (e.g. Primary School Teachers and Science (PSTS) 1991) has revealed that there is a great need for in-service provision in science. In the research described here, even within a well established science National Curriculum, children are leaving primary school uncertain of the importance of plants in ecosystems, and not able to connect learning across the curriculum.
- We need to encourage holistic learning in primary schools, not just because it is more motivating and relevant, but because it has a better chance of reaching the aims of the new curriculum.
- Science is not, and has never been, a fixed body of knowledge, closed to the latest developments and findings. The way of working in science encourages development of those skills that will be valuable to children entering a changing world in the next century.
- Just as science should be making connections between parts of its own subject, we are missing opportunities to make similar links with other subjects, particularly English. Earlier, I suggested that approaches to literacy within many primary schools has become rather enclosed, losing opportunities to make connections to both science and to the environment. English and science should be looking for dovetailing of work, using some English curriculum time to develop debate, discussion and writing that is science based.

## Some practical suggestions

The vital issue is how to convert the issues into good practice in science teaching. While recognising that some of the science concepts involved have previously been recognised as more difficult (e.g. Leach *et al.* 1996), there is also the recognition that good teachers *can* explain complex ideas simply. There is no need to reinvent the wheel. What is being suggested is not a major overhaul of the science curriculum in schools, but the opportunity to teach parts of it with more emphasis on the science ideas that underpin the issues. Various approaches, including debate and enquiry, would assist children's scientific understanding of environmental issues. Most of the resources, including human resources, are already in primary schools. Others, as in the exercises below, may need extracting from other sources.

Primary classrooms often have flexible patterns of working, and the following approach could be incorporated or adapted into them:

1. A teacher-led introduction to introduce children to the main science learning objectives through various approaches, including elicitation, questioning, discussion of an issue and a 'how we came to know' approach. It could include reading a story or a poem. Much of this is relevant to literacy approaches within the primary school.
2. A time for groups of children to undertake enquiry approaches to attain some of the learning objectives through practical investigation and other methods.
3. A teacher-led discussion of the findings of their investigations, using discussion and debate to make the wider connections to both science ideas and to environmental issues. The National Curriculum in English encourages the use of such types and uses of language and in a holistic approach; their development through science would be advantageous.

Any science scheme, whether commercial or self-devised, could be adapted to develop along the lines suggested. Since all primary schools have been provided with the QCA Science schemes of work (DfEE 1998), it might be helpful to focus on parts of these to show how more holistic approaches can be developed from schemes relatively narrow in their approach to environmental issues. The following suggestions are based on these units in particular:

- unit 2B, Plants and animals in the local environment (Year 2);
- unit 4B, Habitats (Year 4); and
- unit 6A, Interdependence and adaptation (Year 6).

In each case, the notes on pages 65–6 are modifications from the teaching and learning provided within these particular units.

The primary curriculum is already very busy; rather than add to it, I am suggesting that some science within programmes of study, such as growing plants, can be achieved in a shorter time by a sensible use of resource, leaving time for more productive inputs, such as those outlined in this chapter. I would also suggest that it is more a change of *emphasis* than a major shift in direction. The links with language and literacy are important to develop, serving the interests of both science and English. The links with geography are also important to achieve the aim of a greater understanding of holistic issues within our environment (see Figure 6.1).

**Plants and animals in the local environment (Year 2)**

The scheme can be enhanced by:

*Links to language and literacy*
- Question them on what they think might be seen prior to a visit.
- Emphasise that seeds produce new plants.
- Discuss what would happen if specific plants were unable to produce seeds.
- Discuss further why they think all the plants had leaves and roots.
- Discuss with them how plants are useful to us in different ways.

*Links to geography*
- Get them to consider locations for the planting of new trees.

---

**Habitats (Year 4)**

The scheme can be enhanced by:

*Links to language and literacy*
- Discuss how we came to realise there were different habitats, each with different plants and animals living together.
- Discuss the different ways animals seek food (herbivore, carnivore, decomposer, etc.).
- Discuss why there is a great diversity of animals, both large and small, found in any habitat that is studied.
- Using a story to introduce an idea. For example, *Dr Xargle's Book of Earth Tiggers* for animal diversity.
- Discuss the requirements of animals and plants to survive in the habitats in which they were found.
- Get the children to debate one or more of the following, using persuasive argument within a debating frame:
- ensuring wildlife is protected during the building of new houses on farm land;
- whether planting new trees in the countryside is beneficial to wildlife;
- whether back gardens are good havens for wildlife; and
- what can be done to prevent animals becoming extinct?

*Extensions to the science activities*
- Encourage greater use of ICT for data collection and for making keys.
- As an investigation, encourage supervised working on aquatic animals in the school pond, leading to reflection on whether predictions were correct.
- Get different groups to focus on one particular animal to focus not only on its range of habitat but on the specific adaptations that will allow it to survive there.

*Links to geography*
- Any of the topics for debate can be explored as part of geography, for example, the effect of new housing on wildlife in the area.
- Explore the conservation of animals in Third World countries.

**Interdependence and adaptation (Year 6)**

The scheme can be enhanced by:

*Links to language and literacy*
- Discuss the theme 'Plants are wonderful!' Use 'how we came to know' that certain plants are valuable foods for us, other plants provide valuable medicinal compounds for us and some are important sources of raw materials for our society.
- Discuss the conditions needed for plants to make food materials in photosynthesis.
- Discuss the many ways that animals use different plants, including food, homes, 'lookout points', etc.
- Tell stories about environmental issues, such as the improvements and development of new cereal species from ancient times to now.
- Encourage children to communicate their results as report writing, using a writing frame.
- Debate the environmental effects of massive tree felling in our countryside.
- Discuss possible effects of air pollution on plant growth in cities.
- Discuss how the processes of decomposition and decay provide a slow release of minerals for new plant growth. Extend this to written accounts of the process.
- Debate the value of genetic diversity on the planet – what are the advantages and disadvantages?

*Extensions to the science activities*
- Provide input on soil conditions for plant growth, including the need for soil minerals by the plant and their preferred pH conditions for growing.
- Investigate as a group the growing conditions for seeds of edible plants such as radishes, carrots, mung beans, peas, etc.
- Make enquiries into which parts of plants are used for food storage, to include carrots, spring onions, celery, cauliflower, etc.
- As a group exercise make food webs from a set of photos.
- Explore a few animal and plant species to relate the adaptations they possess to their survival and reproduction in specific habitats.
- Increase use of ICT to both record their own data and to access data from CD-ROMs and from selected Internet sites to assist their enquiries.

## Link resource

Since several of the suggestions encourage further use of discussion and debate in science, the photocopiable sheet on page 70 could be used to encourage children to develop this skill. The teacher's sheet in Figure 6.1 shows one example of how some of the main scientific inputs could be encouraged in the discussion. It is suggested that children work in groups and respond to both sides of the argument on the sheet – both for and against – and that the teacher then asks different groups to present just one side of the argument during discussion. Clearly, this discussion framework sheet can be adapted, using simpler headings for younger children.

---

**Group Discussion Recording Sheet: Cutting down trees**

**Statements we can make/questions we can ask about cutting down trees:**
- Should trees be cut down in our country? Some say that they should for a variety of reasons while others say their removal would seriously affect the wildlife that live in the woods.
- Trees can be deciduous and evergreen.
- Trees can be exotic or native.
- Trees can be young or old.
- Trees can be in towns and cities as well as the countryside.

**Arguments in favour of cutting down trees:**
- Most have been planted to cut down eventually.
- Many of the trees are exotic species that are poor in wildlife.
- Old trees should be cut down because their branches are unsafe.
- Timber is needed to meet the increasing demand for furniture and houses.
- Wood is still an important fuel for some sections of our community.
- Wood is a major raw material for paper manufacturing.

**Arguments against cutting down trees:**
- Woodlands are a major habitat for wildlife in this country.
- Fallen branches are also rich habitats for wildlife.
- We should recycle paper and wood far more.
- We gain comfort from having trees around us.
- Trees are good at reducing sound and noise in the environment.
- Oak trees have over 400 different plants and animals in them.

**Our decision based on the evidence above:**
- Most trees will be habitats for wildlife and so we should be conserving trees whenever possible.
- We should be recycling paper where possible and so reduce the need to use valuable land to grow trees for paper production.
- We should be planting more native British trees in cities and the countryside to replace those that are removed from the landscape.

---

**Figure 6.1**   Completed group discussion sheet on the topic 'Cutting down trees'

## Conclusions

The implication of limited change to the science within the new National Curriculum from 2000 means that the environment has not been given greater value within the primary curriculum, despite the interests, concerns and limited understandings of primary children, as outlined in this chapter. It is possible to change the emphasis of classroom teaching in science without 'missing out' the statutory requirements. On the contrary, by modifying some classroom practice, the science understanding would be enhanced because it would capture children's motivation and would make greater sense to them by making links across the curriculum. Such enhancement would address some of the concerns that have emerged from several research studies, and would include the following:

- make more obvious the links between the science ideas and geographical ideas when engaging children in work relating to the environment;
- encourage greater use of discussion and debate in science work, both to clarify science ideas and to show how literacy is a vital component of science;
- develop beyond 'QCA-type' schemes which could become demotivating if followed too closely and without sufficient modification by the teacher;
- change the emphasis in some science inputs to help children gain greater awareness of areas identified as needing further clarification, such as a discussion on the role of soil in the growth of plants;
- encourage children to develop their skills in science, especially their skills of enquiry, as a step towards becoming autonomous learners and able to make rational decisions on the basis of evidence;
- encourage children to see more holistic scenarios through a 'how we came to know' approach, linked to readings and other inputs that are sensitive to where the children are in their thinking; and
- encourage the use of questioning approaches, and promote the confidence to recognise that though we can all understand further, scientists are never certain they have the complete answer.

## Useful further reading

*The Blue Peter Green Book*, L. Bronze, N. Heathcote and P. Brown (1991). London: BBC Books.

This book provides lots of useful background, at a level suitable for primary children, together with suggestions for activities.

*Primary Science and Literacy Links*, R. Feasey (1999). Hatfield: Association for Science Education.

A book full of relevant links between literacy and science, including practical science ideas for classroom use.

*Writing Across the Curriculum: Frames to Support Learning,* M. Lewis and D. Wray (1998). Reading: Reading and Language Information Centre.

A very useful publication to show ways to structure writing for different purposes, together with worked examples.

*Environmental Education. A Practical Guide* (1996). Our World – Our Responsibility. Sandy: Royal Society for the Protection of Birds.

This file is full of ideas and activities. It shows links between primary subjects, especially science and geography.

*Wildlife and the School Environment,* (1992). Sandy: RSPB.

This is one of a series of books that encourages better use of school grounds for science work, and provides many practical suggestions for children.

# References

Department for Education (DFE) (1995) *Key Stages 1 and 2 of the National Curriculum (Science).* London: HMSO.

Department for Education and Employment (DfEE) (1998) *QCA Science. A scheme of work for Key Stages 1 and 2.* London: HMSO.

Leach, J. *et al.* (1996) 'Children's ideas about ecology 3: ideas found in children aged 5–16 about the interdependency of organism', *International Journal of Science Education* **18**(2), 129–41.

Mancey, D. (1996) *Biodiversity and Children's Understandings.* Paper delivered at the ASE Regional Conference in Bromsgrove, July 1996.

Millar, R. and Osborne, J. (eds) (1998) *Beyond 2000. Science Education for the Future, A Report with Ten Recommendations.* London: King's College.

MORI (1993) 'Children and environmental action', *Environmental Education*, Winter, 12–13.

Scottish Office Education Department. (1993) *Environmental Studies 5–14. Curriculum and Assessment in Scotland National Guidelines.* Edinburgh: SOED.

Primary School Teachers and Science (PSTS) (1991) *Understanding Forces.* The Primary School Teachers and Science Project, Oxford Department of Educational Studies and Westminster College, Oxford.

## Science link resource: Group discussion recording sheet

**Science Discussions**

**Topic:** _____

Statements we can make/questions we can ask about:

_____

_____

_____

_____

_____

_____

Arguments in favour of :

_____

_____

_____

_____

_____

_____

Arguments against:

_____

_____

_____

_____

_____

_____

Our decision based on the evidence above:

_____

_____

_____

_____

_____

_____

_____

*Chapter 7*

# An antidote for diffidence in teaching art to children at Key Stage 2

*Penny Fowler*

This chapter focuses on research indicating that a high proportion of primary school teachers are diffident with regard to teaching art. This lack of confidence affects many aspects of art provision and perpetuates the cycle of anxiety. There follows a summary reference to the historic context, an outline of the theory of the vicious cycle of diffidence, and a description of a survey conducted with students and teachers concluding with some positive suggestions for confidence building. A practical remedy is then offered which enables students and teachers to reflect on their own position.

## Introduction

Diffident teachers are not sure-footed. They are not certain where to begin; not certain about objectives; even less certain about how to assess the children's responses; at a loss. At best they work from an adult view and fall back on what they think is safe. They do not take risks. They rely on adult vision and, often, commercial stereotyping. They can actually do damage by innocently hurrying the child away from their child's vision and expression so that the child loses confidence and satisfaction with their own expression and turns to attempting the imitation of adult and media expression. It is not an exaggeration to describe this as tragic teaching. It has the precise element of tragedy: heading in the wrong (opposite) direction.

The premise of this chapter – that a high proportion of teachers are diffident about teaching art – does not require a *long* catalogue of research. Indeed, I am relying on the reader's interrogation of his/her own experience and outlook to prove the point. I am therefore simply drawing attention to seminal publications which distil the essence of the problem. Later I will show from examples drawn from surveying some thousand teacher training students and teachers over several years that the problem still exists.

In 1982 the Calouste–Gulbenkian Foundation published the seminal report *The Arts in Schools*. The report summarises the vicious circle of diffidence. The publication also adds the political dimension of uneven provision. It is proper to recognise that some priority must be accorded to remedying the unsatisfactory situation but the proper place of art in the education and development of children is not the focus of this chapter. This is how *The Arts in Schools* summarises the situation:

> Teachers are themselves a product of the educational processes whose imbalance we have been criticising. If they feel ill at ease in the arts and unable to organise these essential experiences for children, it may be because they were denied them as children. This strengthens our argument about the long-term dangers of lop-sided educational priorities. For the cycle is self-perpetuating. Teachers are among the successes of the education system. It is not surprising that they tend to maintain the practices which nurtured their success and *to limit their involvement in the areas which they themselves were educated to neglect* [my italics].
>
> (Calouste–Gulbenkian Foundation 1982: 57)

*The Arts: A Preparation to Teach* was published by the NFER in 1986 (Cleave and Sharp 1986). Although generalised, the findings of the report, based on responses for approximately 70 per cent of training programmes, are perhaps most relevant to art provision. The study found that a major problem faced by arts tutors was the students' initial lack of confidence:

> According to tutors, students seemed to be much less proficient in the arts than in other areas of the curriculum, such as literacy and numeracy. This is not surprising given that many students would have dropped most or all arts subjects during their third year in secondary school. By the time students have started a BEd course it could be five years since their last arts lesson. (For PGCE students, the period without arts teaching could be as much as eight years.) Lack of recent experience in the arts undoubtedly contributed to students feeling less proficient in this area of the curriculum, but it was compounded by poor attitudes towards the arts. Tutors said that some of the students held a very low opinion of their own capacity for artistic expression, regarding themselves as untalented in these subjects.
>
> (Cleave and Sharp 1986: 39)

While the NFER report suggested that, 'On the whole initial teacher training made better provision for art than for any of the other art forms', the survey also highlighted the nature of the vicious circle, the 'lack of confidence sometimes perpetuated from teacher to pupil to student to teacher' (Cleave and Sharp 1986: 83). I focus therefore on building the student and teacher's confidence in the belief that such growing confidence will prevent the cycle of damage and deprivation.

A review of research, *The Effects of Teaching and Learning in the Arts*, could 'locate only one relevant study originating in the UK' (Sharp 1998) – Price and Hallam (1997) – and this study is related to music. The review concluded that:

> There is a need for further, high quality research to identify the specific experiences that can enable artistic development and provide a broader contribution to learning. The research will also need to explore the extent to which it is possible to fulfil both of these functions simultaneously.
>
> (Sharp 1998; 4)

In a paper presented at the BERA Annual Conference in September 1999, entitled 'Craft knowledge: a neglected domain of art and educational research', Rachel Mason (Professor of Art Education, Roehampton Institute) also argues that 'research in art education is relatively underdeveloped' (Mason 1999).

It might have been hoped that long and vigorous debates, recommendations and elevation of the curriculum into the forefront of government policy would have begun to remedy the situation on the ground, at least to an extent where there was an observable if not measurable gain in students' and teachers' confidence as reflected in their own assessments of their skills and knowledge and observation of children's art in schools. It may be that there is an increased awareness of the problem, which is an important first step.

My own informal survey of students and teachers over the past ten years suggests that while there may be a franker and more transparent acknowledgement of the problem by individuals preparing to teach, far too many nevertheless arrive to begin a teacher training course with unsatisfactory school experience. This, combined with ill-informed public and media debate often results in diffidence being compounded by prejudice, aesthetic illiteracy, occasional hostility, defensiveness or resignation.

## The survey

During a period of some ten years, ITT students and teachers were asked to complete a questionnaire (Figure 7.1) which would be likely to give an agenda for planning the appropriate provision of teacher training in art suitable to individual contexts. The questionnaire was presented as an exercise which would assist in negotiating art provision 'for the short time available' in an overcrowded teacher training curriculum. The students were invited to be frank. Responses were voluntary, but there was a 100 per cent response. The exercise appeared in itself to be a useful tool for developing self-awareness. Students in discussion reflected that they were glad to be asked the questions. It was understood that collated anonymised responses might be used for research. Questionnaires were completed by, on average, 80 ITT undergraduate students, 70 post graduate students and 20 in-service training teachers, every year from 1989 to 1998.

There appears to be little evidence of significant change in key responses over the ten years except that it would appear that in 1997 and 1998 the problem has become more, rather than less severe following government regulation of the teacher training curriculum and reduction of time available for art provision. The responses characterised in this chapter focus on 1997 and 1998 when the effects of policy on the teacher training curriculum have been most dominant. I am not suggesting that the analysis of responses is statistically viable. Rather, it is personal and reflective research where the data yield starting points for many enquiries but this present chapter keeps its focus on diffidence and its origins and results. My methodology was simple and reflects my own interaction with the provision, the student response and my knowledge of the students. Thus, although the results are not generalisable and pertain to the context I have described, nevertheless it would be possible for teachers to conduct their own enquiry related to their own circumstances. I characterised the responses into the possibility of three categories: 'diffident', 'partially confident' and 'confident'. In addition to the

1. The NFER found that the most basic threat to primary art teaching was 'the circle of deprivation and lack of confidence'. How do you feel about teaching art?

2. Are you personally a maker?

3. Do you draw or paint on a regular basis?

4. Have you observed children making works of art – perhaps in the family?

5. What have you remarked about children's art in the classroom?

6. Which art galleries/museums have you personally visited in the last year?

7. What view would I form of your personal tastes in art and 'decoration' if I visited your home/flat?

8. If you were purchasing any 'art' to display in a new home what might you try to purchase given a budget of £500?

9. What kind of Christmas cards do you choose to send (if any)?

10. What kind of postcards do you send?

11. What are your three favourite films seen in the last year?

12. What live plays/theatre/musicals have you seen in the last year?

13. Do you make or design any of your own clothes?

14. What school, FE or HE qualifications do you have in art?

15. What was your experience of art teaching as a pupil?

16. When did you last have an art lesson?

17. How important do you think art is for a primary child?

18. Rank five subjects in the order of priority for children.

19. Would you describe yourself as reasonably confident and 'at home' with art, not confident, knowledgeable or ignorant?

**Figure 7.1** Survey questionnaire

collation of comments I employed a Gestalt–intuitive refinement based on the subjective evidence.

The key questions and answers for this chapter are, of course, questions 1 and 18. In so far as the data are susceptible to statistical collection, averaging and viability, the picture that emerges is that still, in 1997 and 1998, 47 per cent of all the ITT respondents acknowledged outright diffidence, 29 per cent were only partially confident and 24 per cent were confident. However, from personal knowledge of the students I would need to speculate that the 47 per cent who revealed diffidence were generally right to do so and the 24 per cent who claim confidence contained a sizeable proportion of students whose confidence was misplaced.

The open-ended nature of the questions offered a more qualitative interpretation of the data. It is not my purpose here to attempt to investigate the implications of the whole survey but to offer you, as reader, some responses which summarise and characterise the focus of this chapter in the belief that you will wish to bring your own agenda of discussion headings to the debate. I shall suggest some.

## *Where the generalist ITT student begins: personal conditioning, attitude, self-view, diagnosis*

Revealing responses to the question 'How do you feel about teaching art' suggest, *inter alia*, that remedies will have to take into account states of anxiety, negative self-image, stereotypical notions and definition of 'artistic' and 'creativity', fear, professed ignorance and, occasionally, alienation.

'Worried because I'm not very good at drawing'

'Apprehensive'

'I feel slightly more confident about teaching art than doing it myself'(!)

'I enjoy creating but I'm not very good at it myself'

'Very unconfident. I have never been good at art and I worry my negativity will affect the children'

'Rather nervous as I always feel I cannot draw'

'Lack of creativity and confidence'

'I'm not particularly confident because I don't feel that I am artistic'

'I do not know much about it'

'Not very confident but if I can make it enjoyable I might feel differently about it'.

## *Where has the generalist ITT student come from in terms of art qualifications?*

A significant topic for debate includes the extent of the responsibility of the school curriculum for under-encouraging art and the availability or otherwise of routes to pre-university qualifications in art on the one hand, and the caught experience and nature of engagement or otherwise on the other. With regard to qualifications the situation was clear. In reply to question 13 – What school, FE or HE qualifications do you have in art? – the most common response was 'none'.

It might, of course, be the case that some of the school or FE students who had followed an art qualification had sought out specialist higher education provision in art. Whether or not that is the case, we know that we are dealing, almost exclusively, with generalist cohorts whose starting point is whatever art they 'caught' in the haphazard curriculum school provision. (With regard to routes in higher education for students with GCSE or A level art, the question now arises whether or not such students see undergraduate teacher training as higher education. But that is the subject of another discussion. Clearly, however, there is a well placed anxiety that the emphasis on funding away from the Higher Education Funding Council (HEFC) to the TTA and the switch of emphasis from higher education/university institutions to schools, dumbs down for potential students the place of teacher training as university education.)

There is still to be refought the issue of whether or not the teaching of all art in primary schools should be in the hands of specialists or semi-specialists. The need to revisit this issue may well seem to be more urgent when reviewing the students' reflections on their caught art experience and the effects and conditioning it had on them. It is not too much to say that some of the implications of the ways in which art is delivered are alarming. From among the responses to question 14 – What was your experience of art teaching as a pupil? – are reflections of experiences which suggest the source of the seed-beds of alienation and diffidence which grow in the pupils. Responses suggested that we need to look at how failing art teachers have attempted, with negative results, to provide what they themselves are not comfortable with. Strategies, generalised, seem to include inappropriate 'discipline', undifferentiated assessment, failure re-enforcement, inappropriate response and lack of inspiration.

'Very boring'

'Had one teacher who marked almost everything B+ for effort'

'Fairly boring, uninspiring'

'I didn't like doing art because it was mainly drawing and I couldn't draw. I used to get my friend/sister to do my homework for me'

'I had a very negative experience with art at school. My teacher used to raise her eyes when she saw what I'd done. But a brilliant art history teacher'

'I liked art, but was not 'artistic''

'I enjoyed doing the different painting things. One teacher wrote in my report 'Has able paint-mixing skills'. This was neither here nor there and I found it really patronising. I didn't sketch or draw at all – lots of cutting out of paper and collages' (this student in responding to what school qualifications she had in art replied 'none (not even GCSE)'(!)

'STRICT'

'Always being told to work faster'

'Intimidating as I was never very good at it'

'Quite intimidating. Worried that I wasn't artistic enough'

'Didn't do much at primary school and at the secondary school did not shine, so teachers spent little time with me'

'awful – creative work was criticised because it wasn't representative'.

It is not the purpose of this chapter to make generalisations resulting from the responses to the other questions but readers might be interested in some brief observations. There were threads of anxiety and perhaps psychological, economic, class or society constraints underpinning many responses. While some were refreshingly innocent and ingenuous ('I like blue'), questions related to Christmas cards or postcards were sometimes treated with suspicion or aggression. Only a tiny minority responded 'home-made'. Other responses included:

'Arty'

'Simple, with a single image e.g. Snowman, holly leaf'

'Appropriate ones'

'I don't care what they look like so I just send crappy cheap ones usually – It's the thought that counts!'

'Anything but religious ones'

'Cheap, recycled ones, modern logos – free at local cinema'

'Not the papery and bad representation of Santa Claus ones and definitely not religious'

'Cute ones'

'Ones that display the area I am in or rude ones'.

For some, the limited catalogue knowledge/experience of films, theatre, art galleries and museums will raise sociological and educational questions with regard to the students' function as a teacher who also has some responsibility for transmitting values associated with culture and aesthetics and who is, consciously or unconsciously, a role model.

I hope that it is also becoming more apparent here that the teacher of art at Key Stage 2 has not only to increase their own confidence in order to provide meaningful art experiences but must find the means of combating the negative effects of a society where art has no longer a key place, where literacy in art is at least as poor as verbal literacy. A recent definition of functional illiteracy in our society took as its register whether or not an adult could look up satisfactorily and find the references to plumbers in the *Yellow Pages*. The study concluded that 'some 7 million adults in England – one in five adults' – could not (DfEE 1999: 8). If we had such a measure for art literacy it would not be illogical to suspect that the illiteracy percentage would be higher. We need also to appreciate that functional illiteracy in art may be more damaging in its way and effect on whole living (quality of life) than verbal illiteracy. This statement may become more meaningful in relation to attempts at expression by a physiologically damaged, accident or stroke victim. It is likely that our ancestors drew and painted before they wrote.

## Remedies

Now to practicalities. The art tutor is faced with the problem of diffidence and the associated baggage of attitude and previous experience from which it has arisen. What are the strategies to remedy this situation, especially for teachers in service? Beginning with the assumption, which experience suggests is justified, that much can be salvaged to the benefit and satisfaction of teacher and pupil, and assuming that the teacher wishes to improve practice, what follows are practical, tried routes and activities. With the emphasis firmly on personal development, a useful starting point is to provide personal responses and your own interrogations of the questionnaire. In addition, a photocopiable art link resource is provided on page 80.

To what extent do your responses compare and contrast with the generality and detail of those illustrated previously? To the extent that they may contrast it may be worth analysing possible causes for the difference. If, by chance, you are a teacher with longer experience and memories of a curriculum of 'the good old days', perhaps your diffidence is less severe or your experience of art and art teachers happier. If you are working with colleagues it would be helpful to share and discuss your responses.

Whatever aspect of your personal experience is provoked by the questionnaire, the essential thing is to acknowledge whether or not the problem of diffidence exists, to be frank about it, to understand why it is important to build confidence and take some steps to accomplish it. It is essential that teachers reinvent their own infant perceptions and devise practice which will enable them to live again through the process that the child faces. This may be in public or in private but must start without preconceived notions of artiness, drawing/draughtmanship, meaning, tradition and sophistication. So, you take pencil, crayon, charcoal, paint, clay, material and make a visual expression or statement or view. Or, take an emotion and express it in a chosen medium. Give the work a title. Record your experiences, your frustrations, your successes, your accomplishments or lack of accomplishment with your chosen medium and your aesthetic judgement of your outcome. Keep working on some pieces and judge whether they get better or worse. Decide whether you, personally, like your representations. Could you live with them? Would you expect them to be meaningful to others? In what terms? Give yourself time. Discoveries may take an hour or a year.

Eventually, take another look at your answers to the questionnaire. Reinterrogate the reasons for your answers. What is the history of your personal education, not only in school but in society, which has led to choices you have made? What do you think about the debate on modern art as caricatured in the media? What dictates *your* choice of greetings cards? Try making your own. Take satisfaction that they may have some kind of originality even if influenced. Enlarge your repertoire of museums, artists and art collections. Decide whether the reason for not liking some works of art is because you do not understand the language, the vocabulary, just as you may find incomprehensible a novel or poem in a totally foreign language. Re-examine your own taste and where it has come from. Do you always go for the easy, the uncomplicated? In other words, re-evaluate over a period of time your own relationship with art by both personal practice, analysis, observation and vocabulary building.

The above may seem trite or a tall order but this is where personal research and experience inevitably leads into assertions based on practice. It is likely that a structured attempt to come to terms and understand the origins and effects of diffidence will result in the growth of some confidence so that you may be safer in having the responsibility for providing the children with appropriate art experiences and practice. You are likely also to be more secure in assessing and planning children's progress, in ways which, if successful, in a Utopian sense, would lead to a community richer by virtue of its being able to express, understand and enjoy itself with all that a truthful engagement with beauty offers.

## Conclusions

If it is accepted that lack of confidence is a condition that exists but that diffidence need not be endemic in art teaching, then a clear and simple remedy is recommended: the teacher must be encouraged and provision made to assist their understanding of the problem, analyse their own position and take steps which will be suggested to give sufficient growth of confidence. All this is simply a beginning to art health. Crash remedies are of temporary value, but reorientation and the slow but steady rebuilding of confidence can and generally does take place gradually, although you may be fortunate enough to have an inspirational experience which persuades you that art expression is natural to the human condition, is enjoyable and can sometimes be transformational. A professional remedy within the context of the whole school is to employ practising artists in schools but the place of artists in schools and their value is not the purpose of this chapter, which is to offer simple and direct suggestions to the diffident student/teacher.

## Useful further reading

*Paint: A Manual of Pictorial Thought and Practical Advice*, G. Camp (1996). London: Dorling Kindersley.

A practical and inspirational handbook which encourages the reader to make their own paintings based on the work of artists and looking at the world around them.

*Teaching Art and Design in the Primary School*, G. Callaway and M. Kear (1999). London: David Fulton Publishers.

A handbook for the non-specialist and specialist teacher to use as a practical day-to-day reference book, with ideas and examples of cross-curricular work which retain the integrity of visual arts teaching.

*Co-ordinating Art Across One Primary School*, R. Clement, J. Piotrowski, and I. Roberts (1998). London: Falmer Press.

A handbook designed to support the primary teacher who has responsibility for coordinating art in their school, 'jargon free' with suggestions for practice as well as photocopiable material.

*Teaching Art at Key Stage 2*, N. Meager and J. Ashfield (1995). Corsham: NSEAD.

Each chapter presents in detail art projects that are suitable for children at Key Stage 2 and provides valuable prompts for teachers to plan units of work for their own class.

## References

Calouste–Gulbenkian Foundation (1982) *The Arts in Schools, Principles, Practice and Provision*. London: Calouste–Gulbenkian Foundation.

Cleave, S. and Sharp, C. (1986) *The Arts: A Preparation to Teach*. Berkshire : NFER.

Department for Education and Emploment (DfEE) (1999) *Improving Literacy and Numeracy : A Fresh Start,* the report of the working group chaired by Sir Claus Moser. London: The Stationery Office.

Mason, R. *Craft Knowledge: A Neglected Domain of Art and Educational Research*. BERA 1999 Annual Conference Paper.

Price, J. and Hallam, S. (1997) 'Can listening to background music improve children's behaviour and performance in mathematics?'. Paper presented at the Annual Meeting of the British Educational Research Association.

Sharp, C (1998) *The Effects of Teaching and Learning in the Arts* London: QCA Authority.

**Art link resource: My private encounters with art**

---

**My Private Encounters with Art**


- Make your own favourite drink, find a quiet corner and complete the questionnaire.

- One week later reflect on your responses.

- Make a list of three action points (e.g. a trip to an art gallery).

- Treat yourself to a drawing book in which to record your sketches, ideas and responses.

- Start drawing with warm-up exercises, e.g. drawing with your left hand (if you are right-handed), fast timed drawings. Take as your subject any objects/artefacts you are fond of. Place them together in an arrangement that you like.

- Produce a private work of art in your chosen medium. (It is very important to feel comfortable here: paint, print, computer-generated, clay etc.)

- Select five works of art you would take to a desert island and suggest what comfort you would find in them.

- Take a 'view finder' to your favourite work of art. Enlarge this section in any medium (e.g. charcoal, collage, fabric).

- Review your progress over an agreed time (with yourself) – 1 month, 2 months, 3 months, 6 months, a year.

- List five achievements.

- Choose your most successful piece of art work and consider framing it and find a suitable place in your home or classroom to display it.

- When you are more confident find a 'critical friend' with whom to share your work.

---

*Chapter 8*

# Design and technology: raising the profile of teaching method

*Alan Cross*

This chapter on research in design and technology education in the primary years focuses on teaching method. Design and technology as part of primary education has received little attention from the research community. There has, however, been interest from a small proportion of those engaged in teaching or those training teachers and working in LEAs. Presently in the UK there is a lack of clarity about teaching methods and, in particular, how these might apply to different subjects, and in this case to design and technology. My personal interest in the teaching of the subject coincides with the gradual re-emergence of the word 'pedagogy'; the art and science of teaching. There have been signs of growing interest in teaching method as a subject to be studied and developed. This chapter shows that there is value in research and through it clarity about what we mean by teaching method. A teaching methods checklist is provided as the link resource.

## Introduction

This chapter aims to review examples of research which have been applied to design and technology education and to show their value for those teaching in the classroom or training others to teach in primary classrooms. The chapter will therefore illustrate the link between educational research and the classroom, illustrating the symbiotic nature of the relationship.

An interesting starting point for consideration of teaching in design and technology is taken from an early proposal for the National Curriculum (DES 1988) where design and technology was dealt with as a sub-section of science. Here the authors candidly admit that: 'as yet there is no wide agreement amongst teachers as to what it [design and technology] should constitute in terms of primary practice' (DES 1988: 72).

Design and technology is about finding appropriate solutions to human needs. It is a subject about human life and about enhancing its quality, e.g. designing and making clothing, a shelter, a kitchen or a bridge. Design and technology is always about dealing in the most appropriate way with a human need (Cross 1998: 4). In order to solve any such problem one has to research the human need, the materials and the tools to be used, etc.. What is required? Exactly what will the user do with the product? How helpful can the product be? Thus design and technology ought to be very much at home in this book on the practical implications of research.

The following section will consider the extent to which aspects of the teaching of design and technology in primary education have been researched and will then move to an example from my own studies. This will be followed by consideration of the implications for teaching and how research and its outcomes might have a positive effect in the classes of teachers reading the chapter.

## Research which informs the teaching of design and technology

There have been few large research projects in this area. What is described below aims to represent the range of writing from larger projects to lone researchers examining aspects of primary design and technology. It should be emphasised that the size of a research project is not necessarily a measure of its worth. Small-scale 'action research' can affect an individual teacher's practice far more than the results of a major project conducted elsewhere, even if it is not generalisable to other contexts. Of necessity, some research is considered which draws from secondary teaching. This serves to illustrate that research into the primary phase is limited but that there is value in considering the two phases of education in an educational research continuum.

### Previous research

An important area which cannot be explored fully here is the contribution to the teaching of design and technology by research into and theory about, children's learning. Ron Ritchie (1995) gives a clear summary of the contribution of the work of Vygotsky (1962), who, Ritchie points out, suggested the idea of the zone of proximal development (ZPD). The ZPD is the area of competence where the child is able to do things with adult assistance, the important step being the move to a state where the child can do these things alone. In design and technology one can see that this would apply to teaching a child to use a new tool. It also applies to more complex concepts such as designing or planning. It could be argued that what teachers require is clear advice about how to move children in and out of the ZPD effectively.

The most celebrated design and technology research in the last 25 years was that conducted by Kimbell *et al.* (1991) and funded as part of the research of the then Assessment of Performance Unit (APU). This included children from both primary and secondary phases of education. In its brief to examine the assessment of performance the project undertook a review of design and technology. The outcomes of that project have had a profound effect on the way we think about design and technology.

First they questioned the view of design and technology as a cycle (see Figure 8.1). This was accepted around the time of the publication of Kimbell's report as a useful way to represent the process of designing and making things. They questioned this from the start, as have many teachers, and considered whether there were not other ways to represent the subject.

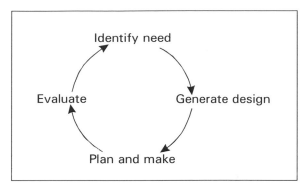

**Figure 8.1** The cyclic representation of the design and technology process

The cycle (presented in Figure 8.1) describes a theoretical way of viewing the subject. Kimbell *et al.* (1991), along with teachers, found that when observing children engaged in design and technology they very rarely saw children proceeding neatly from one stage to another. Rather, children transferred from one element to another and appeared to reverse and omit stages quite rapidly. They wished to emphasise the important cognitive element referred to above. Thus they emphasised the way design and technology switches regularly from work involving the hands to work involving the head; i.e. imaging ideas, problems, solutions, etc. (Figure 8.2).

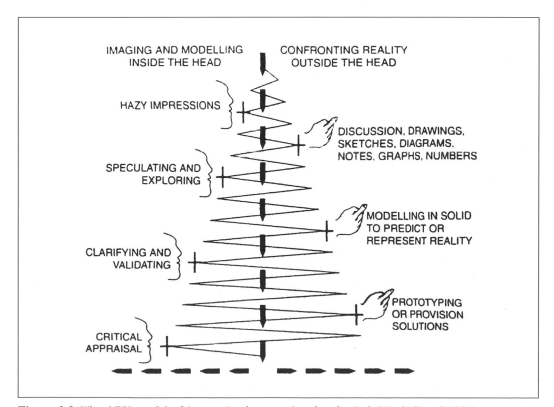

**Figure 8.2** The APU model of interaction between hand and mind (Kimbell *et al.* 1991)

In 1996 Kimbell *et al.* summarised their research (Kimbell *et al.* 1996), pointing to areas such as language used in design and technology lessons, the tasks set by teachers and autonomy of pupils as areas requiring further attention. The researchers were surprised to note the significance of language and how its use influenced achievement in design and technology. They also considered the tasks given to children. Following their trials of different test materials, including different types of questions, they concluded that an important parameter by which a teacher might judge a design and technology task was the degree of the openness of the task; that is the extent to which the task permitted a range of responses. Thus an open task might ask for a safe method of crossing a river. An example which would be considered to be more closed would be a challenge to build a bridge of given dimensions across a span of 60 cm which will support a block of wood weighing 0.5 kg. Both tasks may have a place in the classroom but will elicit quite different responses. These researchers found that the more open the task the better girls performed and that tasks with a tighter definition favoured boys. They also examined the context of the design and technology tasks they gave to children, the context being very important to young children, be it a task about playground equipment or clothing for a well known fictional character or a design for a new litter bin. Kimbell and his colleagues found that girls generally out-performed boys when the context of the task was focused on people (e.g. designing toys for children). In what the researchers called industrial contexts there was a tendency for boys to do better (Kimbell 1996 *et al.*: 15).

A theme of research interest in implications of gender effects within primary design and technology is illustrated by Browne and Ross (1991), who examined the use made by boys and girls of construction sets and by Brown (1995), who found boys using more control technology than girls, who themselves displayed less originality than boys.

Other researchers have focused attention more on the designing and making behaviour of the children (e.g. Johnsey 1993). In a case study based on a group of children whose design and technology activity was recorded on video, Johnsey noted that the making behaviours quickly outweighed any designing. He also confirmed the difficulty of applying any cyclical model to children's design and technology as he observed children modelling and generating ideas simultaneously. The setting of the design and technology task by the teacher was seen by Johnsey to be hugely influential on the outcomes, for example where no time was given at the end of the lesson for evaluation, this important step simply did not happen.

Anning (1993) researched the perceptions of teachers, who she reported were asking serious questions about the teaching of design and technology and finding answers were not always immediately at hand. Teachers were challenged by their lack of subject knowledge and by their lack of pedagogical subject knowledge. Anning referred to 'conceptual confusion', which she said led to teachers giving children mixed messages about design and technology. She went on to give advice about the things that children need to learn to do including: research, image, represent, communicate, cooperate, make/do and evaluate.

## Focus study

Over the past four years I have been engaged in exploratory research about the teaching of design and technology in primary schools. This was informed in the first phase by a series of interviews with primary school design and technology coordinators and by a review of 30 school inspection reports (Cross 1996). This was followed by a second phase of research which examined the teaching of design and technology in five different schools. The objective of the research was to identify the methods used in teaching design and technology. It was expected that there would be similarities and differences from one teacher to another but it was hoped to determine aspects of teaching which characterise the teaching of design and technology as a subject. In a later part of the research, video recordings were made of five design and technology lessons. With only limited space available it is necessary to focus on just two of these as examples. No attempt was made to judge the quality of the teaching, rather the analysis was concerned with presenting a picture of the nature and the range of teaching methods employed.

*Classroom 1 – Juniors*

In this class of Year 4 children (eight-to nine-year-olds), the teacher was observed working with a group of eight children while a trainee teacher took the rest of the class for another subject. The teacher began by reminding the children that they were making a Christmas tree decoration by holding up a previously made example. There was reference to the children's previous experience of stitching, to the skill of sewing and to the fact that these decorations were to be quite small. This didactic theme continued:

> The sheet says 'Design your Christmas tree decoration'. You've got to draw a picture of your design. Now, to give you some idea [holds up a snowman template] you might want to do a snowman. You might want to do this [holds up another example], make a different shaped bauble. You might want to do a Christmas tree [gives other examples], so first step is to draw a design [pause] . . . but as you've got to sew, if it's too small it could be fiddly and so you need a simple design.

The teacher then moved on to reinforce this teaching point related to the need for the pattern to be simple to facilitate sewing.

> I've got an example here of one I made last night. You can see that it's a Christmas tree but it's quite fiddly to sew. Do you think that we could simplify that shape? [Pause] To make it simpler to sew?[Pause] We could have a Christmas tree that is like that (draws an isosceles triangle in the air with her fingers) so that it would be easier to sew all the way round (makes the shape in the air again). We are not going to sew all the way around [partly circles template with finger] because we are going to fill it, fill it with . . . cotton wool or cut up ladies tights.

As the introduction proceeded questions were asked of individual children by the teacher.

> Am I going to draw along the edge or along the fold? Lee?

A series of questions followed about the tools and materials. This session was very much directed by the teacher. She had a number of points that she wished to teach and the context of the baubles provided the opportunity for this. As such this introduction to the lesson appeared to be very successful in terms of the objectives of the lesson. This was very much a focused lesson. At the end of it the teacher hoped that the children would appreciate the importance of motif design for the template and would be able to use a simple running stitch. Several teaching methods were used including explanation, direction, demonstration, and questioning. There was little emphasis on the children asking questions, nor was there much opportunity for creativity. The children could select motif design, although they were receiving quite strong direction. They also had a choice of the colour of felt that they used and the colour of the thread used.

### Classroom 2 – Infants

Here a class of Year 2 infants had been reading stories about pirates and so their classteacher decided to base design and technology on this by asking the children to investigate and make boxes which pirates might use for storing treasure. The session started with a consideration of the characteristics of a treasure chest. Holding up one of the books the whole class examines an illustration featuring a pirate and his treasure box.

> Teacher: And he's sitting on his treasure chest, can you see? It's not a box, it's not a straightforward box like a cuboid, is it?
>
> Child: No.
>
> Teacher: What's it got on it?
>
> Child: A lock.
>
> Teacher: It's got a lock on it. Why do you think it's got a lock on it?
>
> Child: So that nobody can get into it?
>
> Teacher: So that nobody can get into it, that's a very good idea. What is the box made of? What does it look like it's made of? Emma?
>
> Child: Wood and metal.
>
> Teacher: Wood and metal. Why do you think it's got metal bits around it?
>
> Child: It will be too heavy for people to pick it up.
>
> Teacher: So it will be too heavy for people to pick up and take away, OK. Why has it got metal bits around the outside?
>
> Child: To protect it.
>
> Teacher: That's right protecting it, protecting it from what?
>
> Child: So it does not break.

Following this discussion the teacher moved the children to a deconstruction activity where they were asked to dismantle a cereal box, examine its construction (its net), reconstruct it and start to make adaptations to make it into a model of a treasure box. The children were asked to examine joints. The class then moved to the activity and the teacher devoted her time to working with individuals as they were proceeding.

This was a more complex session with an introduction, an initial activity (box deconstruction) and a final activity (treasure chest construction). The teaching methods adopted included: illustration, questioning, challenging and clarifying.

Thus we see in these two lessons a representation of the variety of approaches found in the set of five lessons. They were all very different and yet contained similar elements.

*Comparing the two classes*

The objectives were quite different for these lessons. The first one was about teaching children to design a simple motif which would be easy to sew and later stuff. This teacher had a given amount of time and was very much concerned with making. The only opportunity for design was in relation to shape and materials. This opportunity was limited by the teacher's constraints – i.e. size suggested, example provided, etc. – and lack of emphasis as the teacher did not stress design in this episode. The children had opportunity to draw the shape first but this was the only real element of design. The main objective was related to a number of making skills.

In the second classroom the teacher sought, with the children, to determine the characteristics of the product. This articulation of the attributes of a treasure chest helped the children considerably. The lesson then gave considerable freedom in the choices to be made by the children. Opportunity was given to experiment with ideas. The teacher asked questions, instructed and directed during the period when the children were constructing their boxes. The main focus in the session was making a model treasure chest which included some or all of the characteristics discussed.

Both teachers appeared to be very clear in their objectives for the design and technology lessons. The former directed a structured series of children's activities. The latter had a similar level of structure but varied the direction from the teacher.

In the research each teaching episode was considered under a series of headings, one of which was the autonomy of the child. This was felt to be a significant issue based on the research of others and phase one of this research. The two examples above present different approaches but are not representative of the full range. One classroom of older juniors revealed a high degree of autonomy for pairs of children working together. The example from Classroom 1 gave little opportunity for this, and was characterised instead by a high level of direction and little choice. The children were working individually on Christmas tree decorations with no encouragement to interact or to question what was being done. One or two children did ask questions of a rather functional type, for example, about the choice of colours and the method of stitching.

In Classroom 2 the children experienced varying amounts of autonomy throughout the lesson. At the start of the lesson, shared discussion drew links with literature with which the children were familiar. Here the children were able to interact with the teacher within the structure of the questions set by the teacher

These two lessons were different and represent two different approaches. One would be concerned if children's experience of design and technology teaching was restricted to either of these models. Rather, design and technology appears to need skilled teachers who understand the subject, including an understanding of the pedagogical range available. Thus teachers need to develop a pedagogical repertoire specific to the subject.

## Implications for teaching

In considering the implications for teaching we might usefully ask the question, what should teachers know about design and technology education as part of primary education? The knowledge that teachers need can be summarised into the three areas of knowledge and understanding about:

- design and technology as a subject;
- how children learn design and technology; and
- how the subject is taught effectively.

Although the first two must not be ignored, the latter of these is dealt with here as it was the focus of the research. One outcome of the research is a suggestion that teaching methods can divided into three groups.

- those where the teacher is directly engaged in teaching, e.g. explaining, demonstrating, listening, instructing, asking questions, responding to questions;
- others where media are employed by the teacher to enable teaching; e.g. construction kit, workcard, a computer, television, chalkboard; and
- activites promoted by the teacher where the child might take control, e.g. design and/or make tasks, design briefs.

These categories overlap with some teaching drawing from two of them or all three. In addition to this consideration of aspects of teaching method the teacher must consider organisational matters, including allocation of space, allocation of time, resources available and grouping of children. All of these organisational matters and the examples of teaching method above are items which are variable and which this research suggests can be used to tailor lessons to suit design and technology, the children and the particular learning context. There is no doubt that some advice to teachers would be common to any subject, for example, prior to the lesson:

- determine the design and technology context and how you will represent it/ introduce it to the children;
- consider the children's previous design and technology experience; and
- determine the learning objectives.

There is however advice which is more relevant to the teaching of design and technology. For example, a very important step in design and technology is to determine criteria for the product (perhaps a schoolbag) they are designing. Teachers might pose the question to the children, what are the characteristics of a good schoolbag?

*Developing your teaching*
Be prepared to try new combinations of teaching behaviour and evaluate them honestly. Don't forget to ask how teaching design and technology is similar to, or different from teaching other subjects. Ask the children what they thought of the way that you taught them. Talk to a colleague about your teaching of design and technology. Make a short audio tape recording of your teaching (10–15 minutes). Listen to it and determine how you taught the children in pursuance of the learning objective.

## Link resource

The photocopiable resource on page 92 aims to help you examine and reflect on your teaching. The questions are likely to be important in your development as a teacher of design and technology. They suggest that you should become a researcher of your own teaching, a form of action research very much in the tradition of the reflective practitioner (Schön 1987).

## Conclusions

There is no doubt that design and technology education as part of primary education has developed considerably in the past 15 years. From being a subject taught in only a small proportion of schools and classes it is now compulsory for all children from 5 to 13 years of age. Despite considerable efforts of those running in-service courses it still suffers constantly from successive governments who prioritise other areas. Thus design and technology receives little attention in many primary schools.

The teaching of subjects like literacy and numeracy as a focus of professional development may help to focus attention on teaching, but it is still the case that we lack a shared language of pedagogy. Benson *et al.* (1999) found in the USA that even the best teachers have difficulty describing what they do as teachers. Thus it might be difficult simply to articulate the finer points of good teaching. For those learning to teach design and technology and for those seeking to improve their teaching of design and technology we need a clear language of the associated pedagogy. Thus we will be able to define and characterise better teaching of design and technology and thereby help teachers towards that goal.

Progress needs to be made on a series of fronts: at the level of the classroom, the school and across all schools. The objective of educational research should be to inform the raising of standards without being too prescriptive and thus limiting that to which teachers and pupils might aspire. Thus the symbiotic relationship between teaching a subject like design and technology and educational research focused on teaching can make a valuable contribution to professional development and to the achievement of children in our primary schools.

## Useful further reading

*Coordinating Design and Technology Across the Primary School*, A. Cross (1998). London: Falmer Press.

In this book clear advice is given to coordinators and teachers of primary design and technology. Progression is a theme throughout the book which looks at whole-school management of the subject. There is an emphasis on teaching methods in relation to design and technology as the principal vehicle for furthering children's achievement.

*Teaching Design and Technology*, J. Eggleston (1992). Milton Keynes: Open University Press.

Here Eggleston gives a very useful analysis of the period which saw the creation of the subject design and technology. He looks at the recent history of design and technology as well as issues like gender and assessment of design and technology.

*Understanding Practice in Design and Technology*, R. Kimbell, K. Stables and R. Green (1996). Milton Keynes: Open University Press.

The authors present a number of practical outcomes to research they have conducted during a period of change for design and technology. This book is excellent reading for anyone with a professional or academic interest in design and technology.

*Exploring Primary Design and Technology*, R. Johnsey (1998). London: Cassell.

A toolbox is presented for the teacher. This includes procedural skills, knowledge and understanding and practical capability. Johnsey takes the reader through sections of the toolbox giving very practical advice with good quality illustrations.

*The Journal of Design and Technology Education*, Design and Technology Association, 16 Wellesborne House, Walton Road, Wellesbourne, Warwickshire CV35 9JB.

This journal reports on recent research and curriculum development in the subject of design and technology. Primary design and technology features in every issue including school and classroom-based initiatives.

# References

Anning, A. (1993) 'Technological capability in primary schools', in *Proceedings of the International Conference on Design and Technology Educational Research and Curriculum Development*, Loughborough: Loughborough University Department of Design and Technology.

Anning, A. (1997) 'Teaching and learning how to design in schools', *The Journal of Design and Technology Education* **2**(1), 50–52.

Benson, T. *et al.* (1999) *Action on Principled Pedagogy and Learning Evaluation (The Apple Project)*. Wilmington, Calif.: University of North Carolina.

Brown, C. (1995) *The Primary Technology Project*. Norwich: University of East Anglia.

Browne, N. and Ross, C. (1991) 'Girls' stuff, boys' stuff: young children playing and talking', in Brown, N. (ed.) *Science and Technology in the Early Years*. Milton Keynes. Open University Press.

Cross, A. (1996) 'Comments related to the teaching of design and technology by school inspectors in school inspection reports', *The Journal of Design and Technology Education* **1**(2), 136–40.

Cross, A. (1998) *Coordinating Design and Technology Across the Primary School*. London: Falmer Press.

Department for Education and Science (DES) (1988) *Science for Ages 5–16*. London: HMSO.

Department for Education (DfE) and the Welsh Office (1995) *Design and Technology in the National Curriculum*. London HMSO.

Johnsey, R. (1993) 'Observing the way children design and make in the classroom: an analysis of behaviours exhibited', in *Proceedings of the International Conference on Design and Technology*

*Educational Research and Curriculum Development*, Loughborough: Loughborough University Department of Design and Technology.

Kimbell, R. (1995) 'Uncertain crossing', *Times Educational Supplement*, 20 October, ii.

Kimbell, R. *et al.* (1991) *The Assessment of Performance in Design and Technology: The Final Report of the Design and Technology APU Project.* London: Evaluation and Monitoring Unit, Schools Examination and Assessment Authority (SEAC).

Kimbell, R. *et al.* (1996) *Understanding Practice in Design and Technology.* Buckingham: Open University Press.

Ritchie, R. (1995) *Primary Design and Technology: A Process for Learning.* London: David Fulton Publishers.

Schön, D. (1987) *Educating the Reflective Practitioner.* New York: Jossey-Bass.

Vygotsky, L. S. (1962) *Thought and Language.* Cambridge, Mass.: MIT Press.

## Design and technology link resource: Teaching methods checklist

**Consider your teaching methods**
- How will you share the objectives of the lesson with the children?
- How will you make the context clear?
- What is the context?
- Who are the clients?
- How will you ensure that the children know what they are designing or making?
- Can the children be clear about what the users of this product want?
- Will you be able to place a considerable emphasis on language in the lesson?

**How will you introduce the session?**
Consider a mix of:
- an illustration
- a discussion
- direct teaching
- setting a question or a challenge
- ensuring that the children have time to discuss the product
- introducing a new skill or material
- establishing constraints (limit on time, limit on materials)
- asking the children to do some research

**Will the children design and plan before constructing?** Can you emphasise designing?
Can they:
- design in teams?
- brainstorm ideas as a group?
- come up with a range of design ideas?
- focus on one idea and design it in detail?

**What will be your role in the session?** Will you ensure that children learn to . . .?
Will you ensure that children have experience of . . .?
What method will you apply to achieve this?
- intervention
- questioning
- challenging
- clarifying
- explaining

**Ensure that throughout the whole lesson you draw from this list of teaching behaviours:**
- questioning
- explaining
- instructing
- describing
- challenging
- listening

**In what ways can you give instructions?**
- orally
- written
- pictorial

**How will you conclude the activity?**
- How will you emphasis the learning objectives?
- To what extent will you celebrate achievement?
- Will the children conduct an evaluation of the activity?
- Can the children assess their own learning?

# Chapter 9

# Developing language and literacy through drama

*Suzi Clipson-Boyles*

This chapter aims to demonstrate how drama can be used in the primary school to enhance the teaching of literacy and language with a view to improving learning. Having provided an introductory overview of how drama has developed and changed during the past 60 years, drama's role today is described and a summary of current research areas provided. The chapter then focuses on drama research specific to language and literacy by describing three small-scale studies designed around: drama and oracy; drama and reading; and drama and writing. The classroom implications are discussed, and a case made for the inclusion of drama activities in the Literacy Hour. The link resource provides a flow chart to assist with planning drama activities relating to the exploration of texts.

## Drama in the primary school

### Early background

Drama in the primary curriculum has had an interesting history during the past 60 years. After the Second World War the nation's restored freedoms were reflected throughout society, including in education. Self-expression became an important theme across the primary curriculum, and music, drama, dance and art flourished. In these early stages, the drama tended to focus on theatrical activities such as reading and performing plays, but this started to change. During the 1950s, the work of Piaget (1952; 1958) was highlighting the links between interaction, speech, thought and learning development, and this had a significant influence on the place of drama in children's learning. Seminal works of figures such as Peter Slade (1958) emphasised the key role that drama was starting to play in the education of young children. The emphasis in those days was upon the experiential value of drama in helping children to apply and develop their imagination, language skills and responses to dramatic processes in which they were deeply engaged. In other words, drama was not primarily about creating theatrical experiences for an audience, rather it was about facilitating learning experiences for the child taking part. Alongside new theories about optimising the contexts for the processes of learning (e.g. Vygotsky 1962), the growth of drama continued into the 1960s and 1970s when the trend was to work towards a theoretical base and to justify the inclusion of drama in the curriculum (see Way 1967; Bolton 1979; and references in Heathcote 1984).

## Impact of the Education Reform Act 1988

In the 1980s, growing concerns were expressed about the inconsistency between schools and LEAs of standards and curriculum content. The Education Reform Act 1988 introduced a new National Curriculum that was to have a significant and damaging effect on the arts in primary schools. The government of the time was aiming for a 'broad and balanced curriculum', but the overloaded content of the Orders combined with the introduction of testing in English, mathematics and science meant that, in reality, teachers were excluding subject areas that were not statutory.

Although drama was not included as a discrete subject area, there were some limited references to how it should be included within English. There were also some inclusions in the non-statutory guidelines for mathematics, history, science, geography and history. There were visible attempts to redress the balance with official reports about the value of drama (see Her Majesty's Inspectorate of Schools (HMI) 1990; National Curriculum Council (NCC) 1994; Arts Council of Great Britain 1992) but to no avail. By the mid-1990s, drama had almost disappeared from primary schools altogether, as teachers understandably prioritised that which was statutory and inspected by OFSTED.

## Drama in the new millennium

A review of the National Curriculum in the late 1990s resulted in the so-called 'slimming down' of curriculum content, and concerns about the arts in primary schools started to be addressed. It was hoped that by reducing the content within foundation subjects, there would be more time for arts activities to re-emerge. However, the introduction of the Literacy Hour in 1998 and the Numeracy Hour in 1999 meant that schools were finding time management even more difficult and pressurised, particularly where the 'hours' were both scheduled to take place for all classes in the morning, further restricting the use of shared resources such as hall space and learning support assistance.

At the time of writing, drama is starting to undergo a tentative revival, the first hopeful indication being its more explicit inclusion in the new Order for English (DfEE 2000). This includes a specified sub-section on drama, within the speaking and listening section at each Key Stage. Drama clearly has a relevant place within English, providing children with opportunities to learn *about* language by *using* language in very 'real' contexts and scenarios. However, it shouldn't be restricted to the obvious speaking and listening activities, but should also make important contributions to vital aspects of reading and writing, for example: critical analysis of texts through role play; follow-up writing after a drama stimulus; writing in role for an 'audience' created in the drama; and so on. In other words, drama has an integral part to play within all the strands of language and literacy and this is the specific focus of the chapter.

Before developing that theme, it is also important to stress that drama has two other significant roles within the primary curriculum.

Firstly, drama is a valid expressive, creative and performing art in its own right. It offers a means of self-expression, and gives children an additional framework for presenting ideas, stories, issues, opinions, and other information. Evaluating the performance drama of others is also an important set of skills for children to develop. Secondly, drama offers a powerful pedagogic approach that can help children to learn in other areas of the curriculum by providing concrete and 'real' experiences with scope for discussion, debate and contextualised active engagement with knowledge, concepts and skills.

Obviously, teachers will recognise the tremendous scope for overlap between these three drama functions. For instance, the preparation of a 'documentary' about global warming for a parents' assembly will be linking skills in reading (e.g. for research), writing (e.g. lists, plans and scripts), and science as well as the creative communication skills required for performance! But what research evidence is available to demonstrate that the inclusion of drama in the primary curriculum is contributing effectively to children' learning?

## Research in primary drama

On a purely intuitive level, it is always abundantly clear to teachers who do drama with their children that enjoyment and motivation are only the tip of the benefits iceberg. At a deeper level, drama can help children to remember for longer, to understand more fully, to develop their thinking and language skills, improve their social skills, and develop clarity and confidence in the ways they develop and communicate their own ideas. But, the impact of drama activities on children and their learning is notoriously difficult to quantify. Likewise, it is extremely rare for causal connections to be made accurately because inevitably there are so many uncontrolled variables.

The social nature of drama means that most drama researchers work within ethnographic rather than positivistic paradigms. These offer rich insights into the depth of the impact of drama on children, but tend not to provide generalisable theories based on the empirical data of larger samples. There are also studies that adopt complementary combination approaches (for example, Study 3 described in this chapter) and these can offer interesting evidence for debate, and scope for the development of grounded theory. Research design depends very much on purpose, and although purely quantitative approaches alone are unlikely to do justice to the multi-faceted nature of the subject, (Somers 1996) it can also be argued that small-scale qualitative studies, although important, useful and inspiring, carry insufficient weight to influence policy shifts on the status of drama in the primary curriculum. A move towards theory testing through more structural ethnographic approaches or complementary combination methodologies is much needed.

At the time of writing, a literature search using the British Educational Index (BEI) for studies in drama at primary level produced 104 articles published between 1964 and 1999. It was interesting to categorise these into areas of focus, as illustrated in Table 9.1. The distribution of these categories demonstrates that drama has indeed been playing various roles within primary education during the past 35 years. Several curricular and cross-curricular areas are represented as subjects for discrete study. Likewise, various language

**Table 9.1** Categories of primary drama research (1964–99)

| Research focus | Studies | Research focus | Studies |
|---|---|---|---|
| General (e.g. the place of drama in the curriculum) | 26 | History | 4 |
| Value/place of the arts | 11 | Media education | 3 |
| Teaching Shakespeare | 11 | Bilingual/multi-cultural education | 3 |
| Theatre in education | 10 | Play | 2 |
| Drama for learning/problem-solving | 9 | Teaching geography | 2 |
| | | Moral education | 2 |
| | | Writing | 2 |
| Science | 6 | Gender issues | 1 |
| Reading/story | 6 | Promoting self-esteem | 1 |
| English (general) | 4 | Teacher training | 1 |

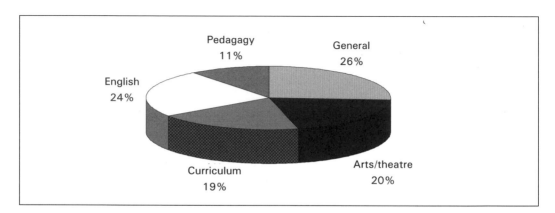

**Figure 9.1** Summary distribution of drama research categories

and literacy categories are apparent. These are in addition to more general studies, studies with an arts focus and studies about the pedagogical benefits. Further grouping of these categories (Figure 9.1) serves to illustrate the (collectively labelled 'English') proportion of studies that represented language and literacy categories.

## Using drama research

When reading research in drama education, we need to be rigorous in our interpretative skills and our conclusions. For instance, we need to separate out subjective claims from empirical evidence. We need to check the nature of samples, the internal validity of the design and the reliability of the measurement instruments. We also need to know, for example, how qualitative data have been coded and analysed and how representative are the voices cited in quotations and extracts. By interrogating the research in our readings, we learn to become more critical and reflective in our responses. This, in turn can help to guide us when we plan our own studies, replicate those of others, or simply use ideas that are offered or implied by what we have read.

# Language, literacy and drama: three studies

Language and literacy are social activities. Not only do they require skills, knowledge and understanding, they also involve complex interactions and responses The three studies described here each explain how the drama was used to enhance the contexts within which language events were taking place. The third study also describes the impact that the drama had upon subsequent follow-up writing activities. Clearly, it is only possible to provide brief summaries of these reports here. Consequently, it is strongly recommended that you access the full reports before following up any of the approaches in your own classroom.

## *Study 1: Improving language in the role play area (McManus 1997)*

This case study was supported by the TTA's Teacher Research Grant Scheme, through which classroom teachers are able to apply for funding for supply cover that enables them to conduct a small-scale research project (usually in their own classrooms). These projects are planned in partnership with LEAs and/or teacher training institutions.

This particular project took place in a nursery class in Leeds and was in response to research that has shown that homes are more effective than schools in stimulating and enriching their language (Tizard and Hughes 1984). A series of activities (for example, the staging of a burglary in the shop) was provided across a six-week period for the children to link into their play in the shop role-play area. The children's language was recorded on video and also tape-recorded, and the results were coded into five categories: statements, explanations/elaboration, requests, questions and minimal responses. As the weeks progressed, the children became less reliant on asking questions and making requests of the adults, and became more instrumental in initiating language as well as using more complex linguistic features such as detailed explanations.

The findings are summarised by the researchers as follows:

- Setting up a role-play area did not in itself produce good language development. The involvement of other adults from outside the school setting, and the planned use of dramatic events were needed to reveal the full linguistic capacities of the children in the sample.
- The children's language was usually of a higher quality when they initiated conversations rather than simply answering questions.
- Talk was poorest when the children were asked a series of questions, if these were open-ended.

They concluded by recommending that teachers' planning 'should build in stimulating events and opportunities, especially contact with adults in familiar, out-of-school roles, so that pupils can make extended contributions, follow lines of thought, and initiate discussion' (McManus 1997: 3).

## Study 2: Drama and critical thinking in the reading process (Montgomerie and Ferguson 1999)

This study, conducted as part of an in-service project at Froebel Institute College, London, set out to investigate the contribution made by process drama to the development of critical literacy in young children. The researchers and teachers wanted to see how exploring texts through a more active learning process (drama) might assist the children in developing critical responses alongside deeper insights into, and ideas about the inferential possibilities of those texts. They hypothesised that process drama would 'elicit from children a more meaningful and critical response to literature than is possible by other methods' (Montgomerie and Ferguson 1999: 12), although they did not attempt to compare their approach with 'other methods' in this study.

The project team conducted a six-week drama intervention programme with children aged from four to eight, although the article only reports on two classes, one of four-year-olds and the other of five- and six-year-olds. Descriptions of what happened in the sessions are given, but details of the research design (e.g. how many children, length of sessions, methods of recording observations, methods of sorting, analysing and interpreting observations) are frustratingly absent. The researchers openly admit that the 'evidence' is opportunistic and grounded in their own observations as participants in the drama intervention. Indeed, the lack of clear measurement procedures makes it impossible to draw anything other than subjective interpretations of the children's responses. Consequently, the findings of the study cannot be generalised, and indeed no clear theory is developed or proven.

The report describes two interventions: the first, with a class of four-year-olds explored *Mrs Wishy Washy* (Melser and Cowley 1982) during two half-day sessions; the second, with a class of five- and six-year-olds explored *Come Away From the Water, Shirley,* (Burningham 1977) during three half-day sessions. In the first case, the text was read and reread to the children who were then offered the opportunity to 'meet' one of the characters. Encounters with adults in various roles from the book during the two sessions led to various re-enactments of the text plus additional new storylines developed by the children to solve particular characters' problems. In the second case, the researchers set out to construct the world of the text; both the realities of being at the seaside with two disinterested parents, and the imaginary world of pirates that Shirley creates for herself. The children developed a whole world of extended story in which they were inventing, creating and problem-solving, particularly centring on the challenge of finding the treasure despite the dangerous terrain! The main findings, in summary, were as follows:

- The approach elicited a range of critical responses to the texts from the children.
- Some children demonstrated language skills that had not previously been observed.
- The approach engaged and elicited responses from children with additional languages in ways that were advantageous to their emerging acquisition of English.
- It provided the children with opportunities to consider a variety of alternative viewpoints.
- It provided the children with opportunities to empathise with different characters.
- The children were not only developing valuable skills in critical reading, but also in critical thinking.

Despite the small-scale nature of the study, it offers teachers a compelling rationale for trying this approach. It provides a detailed description of the approach to replicate or adapt for other texts or age groups, anecdotal descriptions of inspiring outcomes for individual children and useful links between the roles of drama and current research in the psychology of developmental learning.

### Study 3: The influence of drama on imaginative writing (McNaughton 1997)

The aim of this study was to compare the writing of children who had experienced drama sessions with that of a similar group of children receiving equivalent time on discussion work. These treatments were applied to two sets of five children aged 7 to 11 within each of four classes. The children in group A were given five drama sessions, and those in group B were given five matched experiences involving discussion on the same theme. Each age group worked on a different theme: Primary 4 (Year 3), 'Anti-litter'; Primary 5 (Year 4), 'Space Age Adventure'; Primary 6 (Year 5), 'Outsiders'; and Primary 7 (Year 6) 'Adventure Stories'. The writing was then analysed and the features compared using seven categories of focus in the analysis.

The researcher attempted to address the issue of internal validity by teaching all the sessions herself, carefully matching the groups in consultation with the teachers and reducing some variables by selecting for ability, social background, sex, behaviour and attendance. The main findings arising from this study were as follows:

- Considerable qualitative and lexical differences were found between the writing of the two groups, and group A wrote 24.5 per cent more than Group B.
- Group A used more descriptive vocabulary, and used more authentic structures and word choices to convey the 'voices' of characters.
- Group A expressed thoughts and feelings more fully; they also described complex issues, expressed opinions and suggested solutions.
- In 17 out of 20 sets of writing, Group A had met the writing task more successfully than Group B; in three sets of writing, Group B had met the task equally well or better than Group A.

The author quite rightly makes the point that the discussion activities also produced positive results. Indeed, it would be true to say that carefully planned discussion activity is a valuable and important pedagogic approach in all classrooms, and certainly more effective than certain other more passive or decontextualised activities. However, she is also proposing that the drama resulted in even more positive responses. Teachers wishing to try the approach with their own children could very easily replicate this clearly explained study, although it would be important to remember that McNaughton only worked with five children at a time.

## Implications for teaching

These three studies were selected because they demonstrate the positive effects that drama can have on children's oracy, reading and writing. Despite the obvious limitations to making general claims from the studies, it is clear that the children benefited enormously from the activities involved. Whether they would have benefited less, equally or more from other approaches is never easy to tell. Likewise, how can we know if different children would have responded in the same ways? However, the one area of commonality across all these studies (and many like them) is the enthusiasm and motivation of the children combined with well defined positive outcomes relating to language and literacy.

It is interesting to note that Studies 1 and 2 both report that the activities provided the children with opportunities to *demonstrate* language skills in ways that were not always possible during other types of activities. This has considerable implications for how and when we assess children's language. For instance, are the contexts within which assessments take place facilitating the optimum outcomes from the children? Are we restricting children's language output by the types of activities we provide, and if so does this present a danger of misrepresenting their achievements?

Drama provides multi-dimensional language situations that can provide different, and sometimes deeper ways of learning than other methods. There are many approaches to teaching drama (see Clipson-Boyles 1997: 210–11). It is important, therefore, for you to become familiar, if you are not already, with a repertoire of drama tools, that you can use for different purposes. It is also important to remember that drama can be used flexibly in different ways.

### Using drama in the Literacy Hour

This flexibility of drama gives you many choices for use in the Literacy Hour. It is helpful to consider the many variables as you are planning.

- Positioning – The drama may take place during your introduction (e.g. as a stimulus or demonstration), group time or individual time (e.g. writing in role) or during the plenary (e.g. for reporting, presenting or answering questions).
- Time – It may simply involve a five-minute hot-seating activity, or could be 20 minutes writing in role.
- Use of space – It may be on the carpet (whole class) or in a variety of arrangements around the room (e.g. six at a table in a TV Newsroom meeting, pairs facing each other conducting interviews).
- Mode – It is impossible to list them all, but common approaches that would be appropriate to the Literacy Hour include hot-seating, writing in role, interviews, improvisation, enactment, reading in role, teacher-in-role, simulation, and script work.
- Teacher's role – The drama might be created by just the teacher being in role, for example as an alternative means of asking (or getting the children to ask) questions.

### Link resource

It is beyond the scope of this chapter to provide detailed examples of drama activities for the Literacy Hour, but these can be found elsewhere (see Clipson-Boyles 1998: 96–101). However, the link resource on page 104 offers a flow chart that can be used to guide teachers through a series of questions to assist with planning a short hot-seating activity during the Literacy Hour as a means of exploring a text. Hot-seating is where a person (or group) role-plays a character and answers questions from the children. It is a good idea to always introduce the person properly and invite them to sit down, so that you are modelling the pretend for the children! The process can provide an excellent vehicle for children of all ages to read between and beyond the lines, and to analyse characters in greater depth. The photocopiable flow chart is simply intended as a 'thinking framework' to help those who may be new to hot-seating dip their toes into using this effective approach.

## Conclusions

The three studies described in this chapter demonstrate the powerful effect that drama can have on children's literacy and language. Providing 'live' contexts for using and practising skills also helps children to develop concepts and acquire knowledge. The purpose of the daily hour of literacy is to systematise the teaching of literacy as a means of ensuring thorough coverage and consistency. It is therefore vital that the most effective teaching methods are used to deliver this. Drama offers teachers the opportunity to make meaningful and active contexts for this vital learning in ways that will motivate children and produce satisfying results. However, successful drama teaching requires careful planning, good organisation and a wide repertoire of management strategies. Teachers also need to know the range of drama options available to them so they can use different 'tools' for different purposes.

## Useful further reading

*Research in Drama Education*, Carfax Publishing, Abingdon, Oxfordshire. Email to the home page at: http://www.carfax.co.uk

Twice-yearly journal containing research reports and reviews.

*Drama in Primary English Teaching*, Suzi Clipson-Boyles (1998). London: David Fulton Publishers.

This provides a step-by-step guide to teaching drama as part of English teaching and includes guidance on different drama methods, organisation, management and assessment. Activity suggestions are also provided for the Literacy Hour in Years 1 to 6.

*Drama For Learning*, Dorothy Heathcote and Gavin Bolton (1995). Portsmouth, NH: Heinemann.

This provides a useful reminder of the early work of these two significant proponents of educational drama along with additional contemporary thoughts on the further development of theory.

*Drama* (Formerly *Drama Magazine*), National Drama Publications, 6 Cornwell Street, Newcastle-on-Tyne NE3 1TT.

'One forum many voices' is how it describes itself. A useful professional publication that provides practitioners with the opportunity to share theory and practice, express ideas, and debate issues.

*Drama: A Handbook for Primary Teachers*, G. Readman and G. Lamont (1994). London: BBC Publications.

A useful practical guide to drama from pre-school through to Key Stage 3, this book provides planning and assessment frameworks along with some good introductory ideas to assist planning.

*Drama in the Curriculum*, John Somers (1994). London: Cassell.

This book provides an invaluable theoretical base to drama, which is supported with practical examples for teachers to use in their planning.

*Beginning Drama 4–11*, Joe Winston and Miles Tandy (1998). London: David Fulton Publishers.

A very good book for those who are new to teaching drama, this publication carefully explains different approaches to drama with useful practical examples, in particular the use of games and story.


# References

Arts Council of Great Britain (1992) *Drama in Schools*. London: Arts Council of Great Britain.

Bolton, G. (1979) *Towards a Theory of Drama in Education*. Harlow: Longman.

Burningham, J. (1977) *Come Away From the Water, Shirley*. London: Random House.

Clipson-Boyles, S. (1997) 'Drama' in Ashcroft, K. & Palacio, D. (eds) *Implementing the Primary Curriculum. A Teacher's Guide*, 204–20. Bristol: Falmer Press.

Clipson-Boyles, S. (1998) *Drama in Primary English Teaching*. London: David Fulton Publishers.

Department for Education and Employment (DfEE) (2000) *The National Curriculum in England: English*. London: The Stationery Office.

Heathcote, D. (1984) *Collected Writings*. London: Hutchinson.

Her Majesty's Inspectorate of Schools (HMI) (1990) *The Teaching and Learning of Drama*. London: HMSO.

McManus, J. (1997) *Using Role-Play to Improve Nursery Children's Language*, Teacher Research Grant Report Summary Paper. London: Teacher Training Agency.

McNaughton, M. J. (1997) 'Drama and Children's Writing: a study of the influence of drama on the imaginative writing of primary school children', *Research in Drama in Education,* 2 (1), 55–86

Melser, J. and Cowley, J. (1982) *Mrs Wishy-Washy*. London: E. J. Arnold.

Montgomerie, D. and Ferguson, J. (1999) 'Bears don't need phonics; an examination of the role of drama in laying the foundations for critical thinking in the reading process', *Research in Drama Education* 4(1), 11–20.

National Curriculum Council (NCC) (1994) *Drama in the National Curriculum (poster)*. London: HMSO.

Piaget, J. (1952) *The Child's Construction of Number*. London: Routledge & Kegan Paul.

Piaget, J. (1958) *The Child's Construction of Reality*. London: Routledge & Kegan Paul.

Slade, P. (1958) *An Introduction to Child Drama*. London: University of London Press.

Somers, J. (1996) 'Approaches to drama research', *Research in Drama Education* **1**(1), 165–73.

Tizard, B. and Hughes, M. (1984) *Young Children Learning*. Glasgow: Fontana.

Vygotsky, L.S. (1962) *Thought and Language*. Harvard, Mass.: MIT Press.

Way, B. (1967) *Development Through Drama*. Harlow: Longman.

## Drama link resource: Hot-seating flow chart

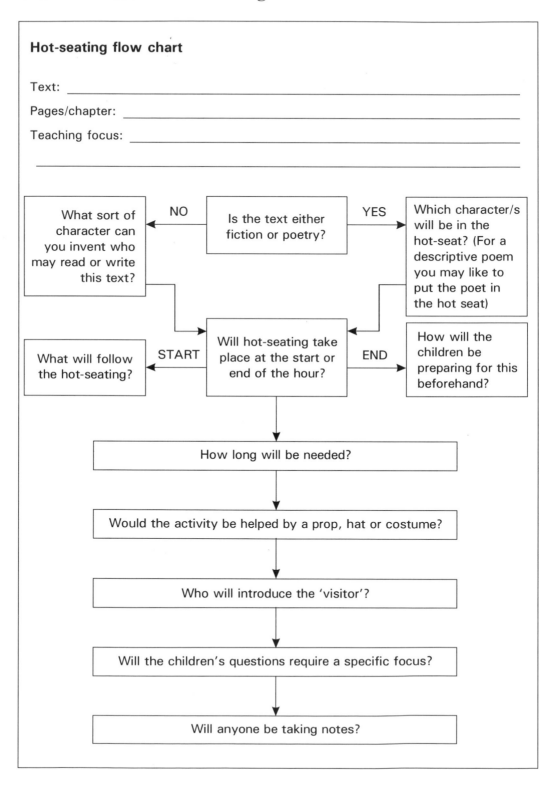

**Hot-seating flow chart**

Text: _____

Pages/chapter: _____

Teaching focus: _____

_____

| What sort of character can you invent who may read or write this text? | ← NO | Is the text either fiction or poetry? | YES → | Which character/s will be in the hot-seat? (For a descriptive poem you may like to put the poet in the hot seat) |

| What will follow the hot-seating? | ← START | Will hot-seating take place at the start or end of the hour? | END → | How will the children be preparing for this beforehand? |

↓

How long will be needed?

↓

Would the activity be helped by a prop, hat or costume?

↓

Who will introduce the 'visitor'?

↓

Will the children's questions require a specific focus?

↓

Will anyone be taking notes?

# Chapter 10

# Understanding, making and using maps

*Michael Brown*

This chapter is concerned with examining how knowledge of research into children's developing skills and understanding in mapwork may support the provision of appropriate teaching and learning activities for them, both in the classroom, and outside in the field. It outlines reviews of a range of investigations into children' understanding of key areas of learning about maps, and identifies a clear progression through the infant and junior age phases to the end of National Curriculum Key Stage 2. Particular attention is paid to what Catling (1979) refers to as 'cognitive mapping ability' and general map reading ability, with specific reference to concepts of scale, orientation and location through grid numbering.

## Introduction

As adults, the ability to understand and use maps is a skill which ranks high in its importance. Hardly a day goes by without us viewing the daily weather map on the television weather forecast or in the newspapers, while news reports frequently include maps to locate their accompanying news items. Our increasing need to travel, both for pleasure and out of necessity in our own country and overseas, make facility in the use of maps essential. At the genesis of the National Curriculum Geography Working Group in 1989, the Secretary of State for Education, Kenneth Baker, pronounced that 'Everyone needs to be able to read and interpret maps'.

Indeed, it has been claimed that 'graphicacy' should rank next to numeracy and literacy as key skills for all pupils to acquire during their schooling. This was recognised by the National Curriculum Council in the current Programmes of Study for geography (DfEE 1999), which require skills of mapwork to be taught to pupils in both Key Stages 1 and 2. In Key Stage 1, pupils should be taught to 'use globes, maps and plans at a range of scales (for example, following a route on a map)', and to 'make maps and plans, (for example, a pictorial map of a place in a story)' (DfEE 1999: 110). They should also be taught to 'use fieldwork skills (for example, recording information on a school plan or local area map)', and to 'use secondary sources of information (for example pictures, photographs . . .)'

(1999: 110). In Key Stage 2, the requirement is to 'draw maps and plans at a range of scales (for example, a sketch map of a locality)'. In addition, pupils are required to 'use atlases and globes, and maps and plans at a range of scales ( for example, using contents, keys, grids)'. They should also be taught to 'use secondary sources of information, including aerial photographs' (1999: 112).

Teaching children to make and use maps presents the teacher with particular challenges. In the first place, there is the need for pupils to be able to relate maps to familiar locations, within their own experience. This skill is developmental, and is linked to the child's cognitive development and personal mobility within the environment. Secondly, there is the requirement for them to be able to employ maps for the study of places which are remote from them. These places may be of global dimensions, and their study may be further complicated because it is likely that neither teacher nor child may have first-hand experience of them.

It can be seen that the development of effective mapwork skills requires a concomitant facility in related aspects of mathematics. It is therefore important that the relationship between pupils' learning in geography and mathematics should be borne in mind when planning programmes of work. Many mapwork skills require pupils to be competent in, for example, graph coordinates, scale drawing or the measurement of angles, and mapwork in turn provides them with valuable opportunities to apply and consolidate their mathematical learning.

The author has always found primary school children to have an innate interest and enthusiasm for mapwork, which has without doubt made the task of teaching the subject both easy and enjoyable. As the skills of learning to read the written word unlock doors to new knowledge for young children, so do the skills of learning to read and interpret maps open up opportunities for enhanced knowledge about the world around them. The application of the cognitive and practical skills of finding out information from a map or an atlas in themselves can provide the child with motivation to explore even further. In addition, the tasks of creating maps by drawing, measuring, annotating and colouring can often result in considerable satisfaction derived through the creation of a finished product, which could in some ways be likened to a work of art by the young map maker.

## Review of research on mapwork

Research into young children's map abilities and their perceptions of maps shows that their understanding is developmental. While young children, even of preschool age, can demonstrate rudimentary map abilities, by the age of 11 children display practical map-reading ability and can draw useful cognitive maps.

Observations of infants show that they can solve spatial problems in their own environments, such as finding their way around. This has been described as their *cognitive mapping* abilities – cognitive maps are the mental maps which they have in their minds, and which they might draw from memory. They are also able to understand and use large-scale simplified maps of their surroundings, and vertical aerial photographs of a familiar place. However, although they can understand and use map symbols, they have difficulty in representing a known place through drawing a map.

In a comprehensive review of research, Catling (1979) defines children's map ability in terms of:

- cognitive mapping ability, which is their capacity to understand the spatial structure of their daily environments in order to solve problems such as finding their way around; shown by their movement behaviour, play or drawings; and
- map-reading ability, which defines their skills in reading and interpreting prepared maps.

Catling argues that the value of studies of map ability in very young children is that it shows children's potential in mapwork.

Studies of mapping skills in children under seven years old have shown that infant children possess cognitive maps, and that by the age of six they can comprehend and use large-scale simplified maps of their surroundings. This enables them, for example, to use a simple map to find objects in a room. They can also understand and use symbols, but have difficulties in following a route shown on a map, due to problems with orientation and scale. Other research indicates that they find it difficult to replicate spatial locations and distributions correctly, and have problems in representing proportional relationships both in size and distance. As a result, they may have difficulties in representing a known area through map drawing.

Early research on mapping with older children (Webley 1976) shows that 6–11-year-olds' understanding and ability to represent environmental information and spatial arrangements develop through three stages:

- *Egocentric spatial understanding* (by the age of six) – Children can produce representations of their familiar world as a series of topologically sequenced landmarks and routes, often originating with a self-object, such as locating their own home on a neighbourhood map.
- *Objective spatial understanding* (by the age of seven) – Children can structure some of the relationships of their spatial environment, but not integrate them into a wider context. They show well developed understanding of familiar spaces, and can represent them fairly accurately, but are unable to coordinate the relationships between them and the surrounding area. Although some of their cognitive map drawing is well structured, the general configuration is not.
- *Abstract spatial understanding* (from the age of ten) – Children's representational abilities show awareness of all parts of the environment as parts of a whole. They are capable of extrapolating routes from within the general structure, and their cognitive map drawings of the local area resemble real maps. Their maps of journeys from home to school show plan views, position and proportion.

## Map symbols and plan view

Children's cognitive maps show that six-, seven- and eight-year-olds tend to employ the use of pictorial symbols. Research by Carswell (1971) and Gerber (1981) shows that children are only able to use map symbols if the meaning appears obvious or is related to their own experiences. Research shows that nine-year-olds can use a simplified map in a familiar environment. It appears that understanding of more abstract symbols occurs at a later stage, because the child must learn to appreciate that symbols represent something real, and are not imitations of reality. In developing understanding of small-scale maps, such as might occur in atlases, true appreciation of meaning and the relationship between symbols may not occur until adolescence. The idea of being able to draw a plan view of features never seen from above requires the ability to abstract information from the environment. This is a similar cognitive skill to the ability to relate abstract symbols on small-scale maps or a globe to a mental image of the world. Such skills relate to the child's level of operational thought.

### Location

In relation to the use of grid numbering to locate places on a map, limited research shows that although seven- and eight-year-olds can use letter–figure grids with confidence, the facility to use all-figure grid numbering does not develop until they reach the ages of 10 or 11 years.

### Direction

Although problems of east–west confusion may persist after the age of seven, it has been shown that a number of eight-year-olds can use a map in a simple orientation exercise, and older children do not generally find cardinal directions a problem.

### Scale

Scale can cause difficulties for children. Research by Walker (1980) shows that nine-year-olds show appreciation of relative size; e.g. they can relate lengths on a map to distances on the ground. However, awareness of relative distance is not the same as measuring and transposing one unit to another. Nine-, ten- and eleven-year-olds encounter problems with drawing to proportion and reading off distances on conventional maps.

There is evidence to show that young children, who have a tendency to be egocentric, can understand relative states, such as 'long', and 'not so far'. However, when they represent distance and size on maps, they show them not by means of an abstract scale, but according to the relative relationships they notice. Their cognitive maps therefore tend to show features they consider to be important larger than those they regard as less significant. Older children, on the other hand, can generally draw proportionally correct maps. Consequently, teachers should aim to develop understanding of proportional awareness before trying to teach about formal scale.

### Extracting information from maps

It has been shown that young children can use their own cognitive maps, or pre-prepared maps in a practical way to extract certain key information where the objective is clear; e.g. to note a symbol and locate its feature, where the relationship is obvious. However, this is not the same as being able to, for example, identify homogeneous groupings on a map, as is necessary to read a climatic or relief map. In order to achieve this, three levels of operation are required:

- symbols should be perceived and understood;
- specific elements in the map need to be abstracted; and
- their pattern needs to be coordinated and appreciated.

This may be beyond the capabilities of children younger than ten or eleven years (Satterly 1964), and so younger children may find difficulty in extracting information from maps to which they cannot apply their own direct experience.

## Specific examples of research

Dale (1971) examined the problems children experience in using and understanding Ordnance Survey maps of their local areas, and discovered that children do not always recognise maps of their own areas. This depends upon the child's own cognitive map, and how links are made with the given maps. It was noted that conventional maps are highly selective and often contain much detail, which may serve as distractions to the young map reader. This is exacerbated by the fact that children tend to look for detail, and not for abstractly presented patterns. For this reason, children find vertical aerial photographs easier to interpret than published maps. It was concluded that children are more successful when actively manipulating maps within the environment than when trying to image its information. In terms of cognitive psychology, the former relates to Piaget's concrete experiences, while the latter is concerned with formal reasoning ability.

Hart (1979) made a study of 6–11-year-olds' experience of place, and set out to find whether children's maps of the local area were affected by their experience of it. He interviewed them about the extent of their movement in the places they were permitted to go in their everyday environment, and then gave them a practical task to undertake. This involved laying out models and toys on a large sheet of paper to represent places in the local environment. He then traced around them, and asked the children to name the places. On analysing the results, he noted:

- a high correlation between the accuracy and extent of the maps and the limits of the children's allowed zones of movement; and
- a significant relationship between the level of spatial organisation of their maps and their chronological ages.

Matthews (1984) researched children's abilities to draw two different types of cognitive maps without the aid of models; one of the area around their homes, and the other of the journey from home to school. His sample consisted of 172 children aged between six and eleven years of age. The research indicated that:

- children show more information on their maps as they get older, but the learning process is not linear;
- they learn about different environments in different ways – even the youngest showed some understanding of large-scale environments away from home; and
- mapping ability and accuracy improved with age.

The research was then repeated using a vertical aerial photograph and a large-scale plan of the local area as a stimulus. The aerial photograph was centred on the school, and showed the homes of each child, together with local prominent features. The map was a 1:1250 Ordnance Survey plan of the same area, with written information removed. In each case, a sheet of tracing paper was placed over the photograph or map to enable the children to record the features identified, and the researcher initiated the task by pointing out to each child their home and the school.

The results showed that more information was provided by the children about their home area with the aid of the map and the photograph than by means of free-recall mapping. It might be concluded that the visual prompts encouraged the children to scan randomly, and so to produce more detail. However, for the journey to school task, more detail was provided for the free-recall mapping task than with the map and photograph. They were also able to record much more detail about their home area than on the journey to school, which may be due to them spending more time exploring the former.

Walker (1980) studied map-reading and map-using abilities with five- to nine-year-olds. The sample consisted of ten boys and ten girls from each of the ages five to nine, making a total of 100 pupils. Each was given tasks in the classroom concerning relative length, orientation and symbolic representation, and a further task outdoors using a plan to follow a route to a hidden 'treasure'. The results suggest that most six-year-olds had some understanding of symbols, and that eight-year-olds had an understanding of orientation and relative length. Walker concluded that using tasks such as treasure hunting was an effective way of developing children's understanding of maps.

## Implications for teaching

Evidence from the above research suggests that even infants possess cognitive maps and have developed rudimentary map skills at the start of Key Stage 1. This provides teachers with a good foundation on which to further develop their children's mapwork abilities in Key Stage 1. Research has shown that there is a clear progression of pupils' learning and understanding of mapping through Key Stages 1 and 2, which has been summarised diagrammatically in the photocopiable link resource on page 114. Although the indicative chronological ages are only approximate, the sequence of learning shown should serve as a guide to teachers in providing an appropriate progression of learning for their pupils.

Effective teaching of mapwork also depends heavily on the provision of suitable resources to support the children's learning. In particular, it is essential that they are provided with maps to which they can relate in a meaningful way. This will usually mean providing suitably adapted large-scale maps of the school and its locality, often simplified to match the children's abilities. In many cases, the Ordnance Survey 1:1,250 scale maps should provide a useful starting point. (Where these are not available, the 1:2,500 scale may be used instead.) As whole map sheets tend to be inconvenient for children to handle, teachers should consider photocopying relevant sections of these maps; copyright permission is required from the Ordnance Survey. It may even be necessary to do a cut and paste/editing job, using parts of adjacent sheets to cover the required area. In some cases the maps may need to be simplified by tracing basic outlines of key features, removing print which may confuse the child, and photocopying the adapted map. Research has emphasised the importance of providing children with opportunities to manipulate maps in the environment, so enabling them to make links between the maps and the landscape features they represent. It is for this reason that local studies provide an effective framework for children to initiate and develop their mapwork skills.

It has also been noted that the use of vertical aerial photographs, to be used in conjunction with large-scale local area maps, will help children to link their cognitive maps with conventional maps. A vertical aerial photograph of the school buildings and the school grounds, and a further photograph showing the neighbourhood of the school should serve this purpose well. Suitably laminated or covered with protective sticky back plastic covering, these photographs should prove to be an excellent long-term investment for the school, and can be used with many different age groups.

An effective and yet relatively easy way to extend and enhance the quality of children's cognitive maps of their local area is to ensure that they are given ample opportunities to explore, as a class, the school neighbourhood. It is therefore important that teachers should arrange to take their children on guided walks around the locality, encouraging them to identify key landmarks, as well as directions and distances travelled. This should further develop their skills in observation, and should encourage them to employ a range of recording and other fieldwork skills. These might, for example at both Key Stages 1 and 2, include adding information to basic street plans, and using a colour-coded system of recording land use and the use of buildings. Experience such as this should also enhance their ability to draw maps showing their personal routes from home to school.

The use of locational games such as treasure hunts, both within and outside the school buildings, can also prove an enjoyable way of enabling children to develop and consolidate basic skills in mapwork, such as those concerned with map reading, symbols, scale and direction. Locational skills can be further developed with the use of a two-, four- or six-figure grid drawn across maps of the classroom, the school buildings or the school grounds, depending on the age and stage of understanding of the children. This can lead on to the use of simple orienteering exercises in the school grounds or the local park, which serve as valuable means to introduce and enhance facility in map and compass use.

Research has also demonstrated that progression in pupils' mastery of mapwork skills through Key Stages 1 and 2 should enable them to include more information on their maps as they get older, gain deeper understanding, and become more accurate in their drawing and writing skills. As they become able to understand and use maps of smaller scales, enabling them to study landscapes of regional, national and global dimensions, they will learn to employ increasingly symbolic modes of representation. This will provide an essential key to the effective understanding and use of atlas maps and globes of the world.

## Conclusion

It can be seen, therefore, that teaching children to understand, make and use maps has many dimensions, and that the starting points for the teacher depend not only on the children's previous experience of maps, but also on their personal experiences of the environment. Some children may have had experience of air travel, so having the advantage of seeing an aerial view of the landscape; others may have rarely, if ever, travelled beyond the bounds of their home environments. Some may have become familiar with maps and atlases through using them at home, or through belonging to organisations such as the Cubs or Brownies; the overall prior experiences of maps in any one class of children are therefore likely to be varied.

Teaching children about maps concerns developing a progression of skills and conceptual understanding of ways of recording information about places in the world around them. This is most effectively achieved when teachers build on the experiences of the environment which children have already acquired, and the cognitive maps they have already developed. Research suggests that this is most effectively accomplished when children are given opportunities to engage actively with maps in the environment, using suitably chosen learning experiences and resources to support them. Where possible, they should also be provided with opportunities to make careful observations of the mapped environment, and be encouraged to use other available resources such as photographs, video and models to supplement them. An appropriate progression of learning may be achieved through starting with the study and use of large-scale maps and plans of the child's immediate surroundings and maps made by the children themselves. This can then gradually lead on to the use of simplified conventional maps of progressively reducing scales, until they become familiar with small-scale maps which relate to landscapes beyond their own personal experiences. Children's atlases provide a good selection of such maps, enabling them to experience and employ highly symbolic forms of mapping portrayed in a relatively simple and accessible manner.

As many aspects of mapwork depend upon children's mathematical competence, opportunities should be taken to ensure some degree of coordination between their mathematical learning and the needs of related mapwork. The current National Curriculum programmes of study for geography now address some of these links.

Although much of the significant research cited into young children's learning about mapwork was conducted some time ago, it is as valid today as when it was first published. However, the current climate of theory building suggests that now, more than ever, some of these studies should be replicated on a larger scale, to develop a more explicit developmental framework to support teachers in planning their teaching of mapwork throughout the primary school.

## Useful further reading

*Mapstart 1, 2, 3 and 4*, S. Catling (1993). Glasgow: Collins-Longman.

A series of four books which address key aspects of map skills and understanding for Key Stages 1 and 2. They include a variety of pupil tasks based on drawings, photographs and maps, with related teachers' notes and copymasters.

*Discover Maps with Ordnance Survey*, P. Harrison and S. Harrison (1991). London: Ordnance Survey and Collins Educational.

This book draws on a range of real maps, photographs and drawings to assist pupils' understanding and use of maps in Key Stage 2.

*Investigating Maps*, S. Montford (1993). Corsham: Young Library.

The emphasis on this book is the provision of activities to enable pupils in Key Stage 2 to make and use a variety of map types.

*Target Geography 3a: Maps and Places*, P. Sauvain (1994). East Grinstead: Ward Lock Educational.

As part of the Target Geography series for Key Stages 1 and 2, this book includes a range of activities related to maps, drawings and photographs designed to develop pupils' skills in mapwork.

*Mapwork 1 and 2*, J. Warne and M. Suhr (1992). Hove: Wayland Publishers.

Two books which address learning about mapwork in Key Stages 1 and 2, by providing information and tasks based on maps, drawings and photographs.

# References

Carswell, R. J. B. (1971) 'Children's abilities in topographic map reading', *Cartographica* **2**, 40–45.
Catling, S. J. (1979) 'Maps and cognitive maps: the young child's perception', *Geography* **64**, 288–96.
Dale, P. F. (1971) 'Children's reactions to maps and aerial photographs', *Area* **3**(3), 170–77.
Department for Education and Employment (DfEE) (1999) 'Geography', *The National Curriculum: Handbook for Primary Teachers in England: Key Stages 1 and 2*. London: The Stationery Office.
Gerber, R. (1981) 'Young children's understanding of the elements of maps', *Teaching Geography* **6**(3), 128–33.
Hart, R (1979) *Children's Experience of Place*. New York: Irvington.
Matthews, M. H. (1984) 'Environmental cognition of young children: images of journey to school and home area', *Transactions of the Institute of British Geographers*, New Series **9**(1), 89–105.
Satterley D. J. (1964) 'Skills and concepts involved in map drawing and map interpretation', *New Era* **45**, 264.
Walker, R. J. (1980) 'Map using abilities of 5 to 9 year old children', *Geographical Education* **3**(4), 545–54.
Webley, P. (1976) 'Children's cognitive maps'. Paper presented at the BPS Social Psychology Conference, York, September.

# Geography link resource: Mapping stairway

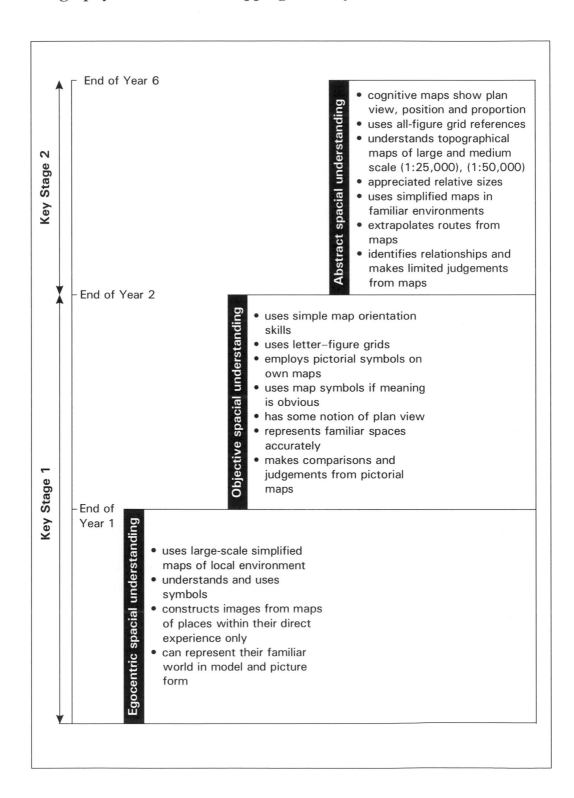

*Chapter 11*

# Telling the truth? Using stories to teach history to young children

*Peter Vass*

This chapter discusses the importance of using stories when teaching history in primary schools. It explores the idea that stories can help children not only better understand history, but also relate past events to their own experiences in the present. A small-scale piece of qualitative research is described in which a group of six Year 2 children were told historical stories in a whole-class teaching session and then interviewed individually. The three clear themes that emerged from the data were:

- the veracity of previously held knowledge;
- the 'all things are possible' past; and
- the persuasiveness of the story-teller.

The chapter describes these themes and considers their implications for classroom practice. Finally a photocopiable teaching session is provided to assist classroom practitioners in this approach.

## Introduction

The introduction of National Curriculum history in 1991 refocused attention on what had been for decades the life-blood of history for children: the historical story. The selection of stories suitable for five- to seven-year olds has always presented problems for curriculum writers, the most recent contribution providing a model of planning around two stereotypical histories: the Great Fire of London and Florence Nightingale (DfEE 1998). As various bodies wrote and rewrote National Curriculum history (DES 1991; NCC 1993; SEAC 1993; DfE 1995) they were consistent in their recognition of story as a valuable and viable aspect of teaching history to young children, but consistently failed to recognise it as a version of reality through which children could better understand the present and their own lives.

As adults we often assume that the transitions we expect children to make into far off times can take place comfortably and easily. This is seldom the case. I recently watched a student teach a very good lesson on Ancient Greece to her Year 3 class which ended with her telling the story of Theseus and the Minotaur. It was well told with plenty of description of sea journeys in triremes, Minos's palace at Knossus and, of course, the puzzling maze itself. The story climaxed with the duel between the hero, Theseus, and the monstrous Minotaur and the slaying of that gruesome beast. Such was the power of the narrative and the student's telling of it, that the children left the classroom in something of a daze, not sure what to make of this remarkable piece of 'history' they had been given. I questioned the student afterwards on how she felt the session had gone. Very well, she thought. The children had been attentive throughout and seemed to be engrossed in the story. But, I asked her, what of Ancient Greece? What impression did she think the children had made of that place? It was a myth, she explained, they knew it wasn't true. How did she know that? I asked her. Silence. And here was the rub. The past is a mysterious place to young children. We teach of a world in years gone by inhabited by gigantic monsters, some of which flew, others that wallowed in luxuriant swamp and some that swam in shallow seas. If we expect children to believe in dinosaurs, why not minotaurs?

## Historical stories for children: a continuing tradition

Much has been written recently on the importance of story in young children's learning of history (Hoodless 1998; Bage 1999). The fact that a prescribed history education for five- to seven-year-olds is a relatively recent phenomenon does not mean that history was not being taught in schools before 1991. The original History Order (DES 1991) recognised the role historical sources can play in the education of five- to seven-year-olds but it was to story that greater emphasis was given in the non-statutory guidance (DES 1991: Section D). The SATs material for Key Stage 1 history cited 'History from Stories' as an assessable aspect of the history curriculum (SEAC 1993) and the NCC Key Stage 1 book, (NCC 1993) presented valuable ideas on using stories. I have used a statement from this document as a rationale for using story ever since:

> Story has long been considered an appropriate method of teaching history to infants. A good, well-told story, commands attention and can lead to discussion, question and answer. The attraction of story lies in its narrative power, through which it appeals to children's curiosity, emotions and imagination. It is an effective way of extending vocabulary, introducing new knowledge and addressing moral issues. Listening to, retelling and creating stories are activities which appeal to children of all abilities.                              (NCC 1993: 33)

The revised version of the National Curriculum (DfE 1995) made less overt reference to story but it was implicit in all of the areas of study for Key Stage 1. However, what is still lacking today, and continues to need refining, is an understanding of the function it has in helping children draw closer to the reality of the past.

### *Versions of reality – another use of story*

There is much evidence that story has become accepted as a valued and valuable aspect in young children's learning of history (Vass 1996). However, does hearing or reading an historical narrative bring children closer to the reality of the past? Does a story give them a true impression of the way the past really was? Clearly, it is too much to expect reality in these terms to be evident to five- to seven-year-olds but it does raise some important questions on the purpose of telling historical stories to children. Is it to give them a flavour of the historical past or is it to present a piece of dramatic action to engage, engross or simply entertain them – history as a sort of value added? If a story is to have an educational purpose in the learning of history it must be able to do both. However, when the medium and the message become tightly enmeshed, is it possible for children to distinguish between fact and fiction? This is a difficult enough task for adults. Many books and films that achieve best-seller or blockbuster status are set in history with both real and invented characters and events included to create the 'look of the past', as Natalie Zemon Davies (Zemon Davies 1987) has described it. Our enjoyment of books and films does not derive purely from an interest in history but from our emotional involvement with characters and plot. To spend time trying to distinguish between reality and invention would be to disengage from the setting the writers and film-makers have created for us; as in films, as in novels, as for adults, as for children. When children hear stories they do not spend time deliberating on whether Theseus and the Minotaur were fact, fiction or a mixture of both. Their involvement depends on the degree to which the stories sustain their interest and the level of emotional engagement they generate. However, if children are expected to be gaining insights into a historical past, then emotional involvement cannot be the only criterion by which a successful story should be measured. They also need to possess qualities that persuade children of their reality. As all early years teachers know, children at this age have a limited experience of the present and even less well defined knowledge of the past. The demarcations between fantasy and reality, fact and fiction, are grey indeed. I decided to make this area the subject of my research.

## The research

### The sample

The research question I set myself was to ascertain whether it is possible to determine qualities in historical stories that persuade children of their veracity. I based my study on the responses of a group of six children to three historical stories set in the distant past in order to examine notions of difference and strangeness and test out their believability. I told them on three separate weeks around a unifying theme of kings and queens. This was not a conscious decision on my part to teach 'top down' history but was determined by the range of choice I had when selecting material. If I was to test children's perceptions of historical reality, I needed to select three stories with varying degrees of veracity attached to them. For this reason I chose a 'real' historical story: the rivalry between King Stephen and Queen Mathilda in the twelfth century, the legend of King Richard I and Blondel and the myth of King Arthur's accession. Of course, a story is a story, and these definitions could not be adhered to precisely. Some are closer to the actual events than others, and none can claim veracity as their absolute preserve.

The children I chose for the study were a representative sample from a mixed ability class of Year 2 children in a large urban primary school outside Oxford. They were an even mix of boys and girls drawn from able, average and less able groups, as determined by the teacher. I told the stories to the whole class and, after each session, interviewed the group on the story they had just heard. Each story lasted between 15 and 20 minutes, and was told on the carpet in their classroom.

## Methodology

I adopted a variation on the practitioner/researcher model of classroom interaction. Although the programme was designed not to precipitate change as such, but merely to gauge the responses of the children, I felt my personal intervention would be necessary to ensure uniformity of experience and maintain control over the material and its delivery.

I adapted the stories for the children to ensure there was sufficient plot, drama and narrative to sustain the interest of my audience. This process was not without its difficulties as I endeavoured to balance the literal and the historical elements. How much should I concede to history in order to make the story truthful? How much should I concede to literature to give the story appeal? The balance between these elements is a delicate one and has been the subject of much contemporary debate. Hayden White (1987), the American philosopher of history, argues that historians have always used literary forms and style to write their histories, and that the borders between fact, fiction and interpretation are very imprecise. Historical facts have never been clear, distinct and irrefutable. However, questioning them should not weaken history as a discipline or limit is parameters as a school subject, but rather offer opportunities to consider their veracity and give children a clearer idea of the historical process.

As I was investigating the nature of children's belief and understanding I needed an immediate response to the story after it had been told. I negotiated to see each child individually within five minutes of the story's completion. I chose the mechanism of the semi-structured interview, a technique now widely advocated and practised (Drever 1995; Scott and Usher 1999). The main advantage was that it gave me the quality of information I required to answer my research question as opposed to a method that would generate more data over which I would have less control. I had certain key questions – 'Did you enjoy the story?', 'Do you think it really happened?' – which I would ask all children at some time during the interview, but I mainly used children's answers to pick up points through which I would question their ideas. For example:

PV: What else made you think the story really happened?

Nathan: The armies and the war.

PV: Do we still have wars in England today?

Nathan: Not in England, but there are still wars.

PV: What would it have been like in England, do you think, with a war going on?

Nathan: It would be bad. There would be houses knocked down and there would be bombs and there would be people evacuated and there would be armies firing guns and tanks.

I had previously acquainted myself with the children and confirmed they were happy to answer some questions and have them recorded. I avoided, when I could, the use of the word 'true', for this has many different connotations and meanings for six-year-olds. I chose, instead, to ask 'Do you think the story really happened?' This would produce a 'yes' or 'no' answer which could then be investigated further in order to discover what persuaded them to hold that view. The data I collected consisted of 18 separate interviews (three stories told to six children), each transcribed text being between 40 and 50 responses long, with approximately 20 questions and answers. The business of sifting and processing the data went through four distinct stages:

- transcribing taped dialogue into numbered lines of questions and responses;
- determining themes and categories;
- collating responses to most common themes; and
- reorganising categories.

After reading through the transcripts several times, it became apparent that certain features were materialising that were to become, on analysis, key indicators of the children's thinking.

## Findings

My first list of identified themes was:

- the veracity of previously held knowledge;
- The 'all things are possible' past;
- the persuasiveness of the story-teller;
- associations between past and present;
- doubts and uncertainties;
- identifying through emotional engagement;
- certainties and rational explanations;
- the mysterious past; and
- mythic thinking.

Responses were coded and counted to determine frequency and subsequent categorisation. Some were unique and, although interesting, not significant or representative to thinking as a whole, e.g. Karen cited her disbelief in Merlin's 'tricks' and came up with rational explanations of how they might have been done. Many categories could be accommodated within others. Mythic thinking, for example, was included in the 'all things are possible' past as there were clear overlaps. I eventually arrived at three categories which had a direct bearing on explaining why the historical stories I had told were almost universally believed:

- the veracity of previously held knowledge;
- the 'all things are possible' past; and
- the persuasiveness of the story-teller.

*The veracity of previously held knowledge*

It is important to remember that young children possess considerable historical knowledge drawn from their parents, grandparents, television programmes, films, books, comics and magazines and this knowledge was used by them to weigh the credentials of the stories. Story 1 was most productive in this respect with four out of six children citing examples. Nathan compared the powers of kings and queens today with those in medieval times, Alex drew on his knowledge of ships and Alicia provided a fascinating example of camouflage which convinced her that Mathilda's escape from Oxford Castle in a white cloak on a snowy day was probably true.

> PV: What about the part of the story where the queen escapes from the castle, do you think that happened?
>
> Alicia: Yes, I think that did.
>
> PV: Why do you think that?
>
> Alicia: Because I can imagine because I've done something like that when I hid from Mummy and Daddy.
>
> PV: What did you do?
>
> Alicia: Well, I was in pink pyjamas and I hid on my pink duvet and they walked in and didn't know I was there.
>
> PV: That's brilliant, just like the queen in the snow then, wearing her white cloak in a snowy field.
>
> Alicia: Yes, I can imagine that.

In the same way that children were using their knowledge and experience of the present to confirm or reject the story, there were also instances of them calling upon their emotions when making decisions about right and wrong, truths and lies. For many years teachers have recognised this affective thinking as an important mode of learning when logico-deductive systems are still at an early stage. Kieran Egan cites this as a 'mythic' mode of thinking in which 'the child's world is full of entities charged and given meaning by those things the child knows best: love, hate, joy, fear, good, bad' (Egan 1986: 12). In the story of Stephen and Mathilda, for example, there is the incident of the 'sinking of the White Ship', in which Henry I's son is drowned. This had a considerable emotional impact on Alex, who compared the story to watching the film *Titanic*. He clearly understood loss and tragedy, not merely as a feature of a historical story, but as a human experience with which he could empathise.

> Alex: It was sad, when the boy drowned.
>
> PV: Yes it was, wasn't it, but when boats sink these things happen, don't they, but it is very sad, you're right. Why did you think about that?
>
> Alex: I was thinking about the *Titanic*. That was sad.
>
> PV: Did the film make you sad?
>
> Alex: Yes it did. I cried a bit, so did my mum. I've got the story about it. My baby brother cried a bit too.

Through these stories children became aware of a past; a past that, in many ways, is not far removed from the realities of their present-day experience. There were differences in context, situation and settings which were often mysterious, occasionally bewildering, but the essential 'humanness' of the story – the problem, the tragedy, the comedy and the irony – linked past to present in a meaningful way. Historical narratives are peculiar, particular in time and place, but there are within them universal realities. Because the past is complex, because reality is idiosyncratic, chaotic, difficult to fathom and impossible to rationalise, it is the structure that narrative provides that gives the young child the best chance of making sense of it. Even when the investigation is intellectual or theoretical, the temptation is always to employ a narrative paradigm to make it understandable.

Jerome Bruner has been foremost in theorising on this subject and describes it as the 'narrative construal of reality' (1996). He argues that the quest for truth can only be investigated scientifically and logically as it is within a paradigmatic mode of knowing, but it would be wrong to think that we live our lives this way. Our construction of reality, and I include children in this, depends on the stories we are told, our interpretation and reaction to them and our weighing of their significance, which determines the degree to which they become part of our world view. For young children the historical narratives they assimilate, whether from school, family, television or other sources make sense to them, not only because they have associations with their own experience, but also because they match the realities they are learning.

### The 'all things are possible' past

Perhaps the most interesting aspect of the study was to reveal the ways in which children rationalised the stories in order to perceive them as real events. One particular feature was the belief that things were possible a long time ago that are no longer possible today. This was particularly marked in the story of King Arthur where magical events like the sword in the stone, the hand appearing from the lake bearing Excalibur and Merlin's magic were believed to have actually occurred. Nathan rationalised some aspects of the Arthur story in this way:

> Nathan: Yes, he (Arthur) needed to have a magic sword if he was going to be king so it would come to him in a magic way. It would have been in those days.
>
> PV: In those days, yes. Do you think things like that could happen today?
>
> Nathan: No.
>
> PV: Why not?
>
> Nathan: We don't have the magic.
>
> PV: Why don't we?
>
> Nathan: Because they only had it in the olden days.
>
> PV: Did everybody have it?
>
> Nathan: No, only people like magicians, like Merlin.

PV: What could they do?

Nathan: All sorts, like disappearing and saving people and doing spells.

PV: Do people do spells today?

Nathan: No.

PV: But we have magicians today, don't we?

Nathan: Yes, but they don't do spells.

As part of his theory of child development Egan proposes that 'learning at the mythic stage involves making sense of the unknown world without in terms of the known world within' (Egan 1986: 12). He argues that, before the age of seven, children make sense of the world through mental imaginings prompted, more often than not, by emotional and moral experience. The choice of the word 'mythic' is interesting in this context. Egan uses it because he believes there is similarity in the thinking used by children at this age and that of myth-using people. By this he asserts that the explanations made are both logical and reasonable in the context of the culture they serve and this is also true of ancient cultures and civilisations who sought to understand the way the world worked through their own myths and stories. These rationales have an interesting link with the explanations of magical Arthurian times made by the children I interviewed. The truth of those times was mythological, so it is logical for children to see them in those terms today. When the children talked of magic, they were trying to imagine a time when things like swords appearing from lakes may or may not have happened, but might have been believed to have happened through a shared mythic sense which united and identified its believers.

The systems through which the children categorised and rationalised their experiences were often personal, idiosyncratic, but 'made sense' to the user. The six-year-olds I talked to were at an interesting age in terms of their thinking for some were beginning to make clear distinctions between what they understood to be possible and impossible. They were forming ideas about the world outside their experience and relating these to their thinking, or, in Egan terms, making the transition from the mythic stage, which coincides with the perception that 'the world is autonomous, is separate, and fundamentally different from the child' (Egan 1986: 29).

### The persuasiveness of the story-teller

PV: What did you like about it (the story)?

Alicia: Well, I liked how you made the story come alive through the words and the adjectives.

It has long been recognised that teachers have a powerful mode of communication at their fingertips when employing story-telling as an educational tool (Egan 1988). However, it is the mode of communication, 'the telling', that can make all the difference between whether a story is believed or not by young children. I entered the classroom as a trusted adult, introduced by the other trusted adult, the teacher herself, I was, in effect, their surrogate teacher, and teachers are honest people, purveyors of truth; they don't tell children lies. I spoke as a figure of authority and employed the techniques of an actor to gain and sustain my audience's attention. I also made the children passive receptors of the stories. I did not encourage questions, discussions or other interactions. This was important for the purpose of my research as I wanted them to make their judgements purely on what they heard, but, without this exchange, the children had only my story on which to make their judgements and I was a powerful medium for communication, one they were unlikely to dispute. In Nathan's words, I made the story sound true.

> PV: Was there anything else that made you think it was a real story?
>
> Nathan: Eh . . . the way you told it.
>
> PV: The way I told it?
>
> Nathan: Yes, you made it sound true.

It is foolish to pretend that story-tellers do not artificially shape historical events. Husbands, writing as devil's advocate, identifies its faults:

> Story-tellers can oversimplify; they sketch characters as caricatures and complex situations as archetypes of good and evil; they impose coherence where there is none; they impose structure; . . . they impose on their stories a logic of causation and of sequence which draws their listeners from the point they have identified as their beginning, securely to the point they identify as the end.                                                   (Husbands 1996: 49)

The children's readiness to accept the veracity of the stories was a result of my efforts to make the stories accessible to them and this presented a problem in their learning of history. The events in my stories needed to be ordered and sequenced to make them logical and understandable for my six-year-old audience; more complex elements had to be omitted, the language made appropriate. However this process can distort and reduce the story to such a degree that the remaining historical content becomes negligible. The original sources do not always record events with sufficient narrative flow, thus making them sound disjointed. I, therefore, included fictional elements to make the transitions smoother. The purpose behind my efforts was honourable: it was to make my stories, my histories, as interesting as possible. When I told them, my performance was as professional as I could make it. The language, the tone of my voice, the gestures I included created dramatic intensity, humour, irony, puzzle and problem. All these elements combined to give the children a powerful and engaging experience of history but it can be argued that it also distanced them from the realities of the past.

## Implications for teaching

### Historical stories in the classroom

Stories are formidable teaching instruments and, in the hands of skilled story-tellers, can be enormously persuasive. The shared experience of story can also create a climate of calm and sensitive exchange, and provide a platform for mutual respect and harmony.

However, in terms of the teaching of history, there must be more than just the story. As I mentioned in my introduction, it is easy to let the story speak for itself, but, if we are to use it for historical purposes, it must be considered, discussed and analysed by the children. It must become the subject of scrutiny, its authenticity questioned, its credentials examined. In this way it can shed light on the historical past it represents.

### Story as a version of the past

The recent scheme of work for history published by the DfEE (1998) urges teachers to make meaningful links between history and literacy, recognising that 'history lessons can also provide valuable opportunities to reinforce what children have been doing during the literacy hour and apply it in a different context' (DfEE 1998: 16). Many of the units utilise historical stories. For example, Unit 5 is entitled, 'How do we know about the Great Fire of London?' Teachers are advised to read or tell the story of the fire and then ask questions of a factual nature: 'Why did the fire start?', 'Why did it end?', 'What were the results?', and so on. One activity requires the children to consider the question, 'How do we know about the Great Fire?', introducing them to the idea of an eyewitness and the reliability of the diary of Pepys as a source of historical evidence.

Tasks like this are fine up to a point, but, for six-year-olds, the truthfulness of a story needs to be examined from their own perspective as much as from historical witnesses and, to this end, I would wish to include an activity which considered the story as a story, and what marked it as true or false in the children's eyes. This is no mere academic exercise. The historical stories that teacher tell are often based on second or even third testimony; a version of events reconstructed by a twentieth-century historian and then diluted for the taste of six-year-olds. Of course, this is the only sensible course to take, for no historical story is ever more than a version of events and often a sanitised, censored, expedient version, particularly when organised for children. Early questions, therefore, should not only be about why and where did an event start, but also how accurate is it. In this way, stories that are less historically reliable, like Arthur and Richard and Blondel, are open to scrutiny as well. To their credit, the writers of Unit 5 include some very good activities in respect of establishing the credentials of the Great Fire as an event, like asking children to ponder on whether a diary is a work of fact or a work of fiction. However, I would suggest an activity to come between the recounting of the story and the consideration of the evidence which will help the children understand a little of what story does to history.

At the age of seven, children are often thrust into dim and distant corners of time and place with very little preparation being made to help them to enter these fantastic worlds. Teachers must ensure that children recognise that their inhabitants were human too and could be as like them as the people in the next street or town. Many children will find this exercise difficult at first. They are not using historical evidence to make their decision but merely responding to how persuasive the story is. A reasonable analogy might be that, after watching *Schindler's List* or reading Pat Barker's *Regeneration*, we have to decide which events and characters were real and which have been introduced to 'oil the plot'. However, an essential part of the analysis of any story that is being used to teach children history is whether it is convincing or persuasive at its own level for this is how we, as its audience, first receive it intellectually and emotionally.

## Link resource

The first part of the session requires the teacher to read, or preferably tell, a historical story to children. I would then suggest an activity which passes through the several stages of development, based on different levels of questioning. They are provided here on a photocopiable page (p. 127) for reference and planning and can be applied generically to both key stages.

## Conclusions

Story, although still widely practised in the primary schools, is an underused resource for learning history. The opportunities are wide and various. Hilary Claire (1996) puts together a powerful argument for using historical stories to introduce multicultural and non-sexist issues to children. There have been some important recent contributions on English and primary school history (Hoodless 1998) and the utilising of story for historical purposes is now gradually being recognised (Bage 1999). However, there is still important work to be undertaken in this area. Questions of veracity lie at the heart of all historical study and children need to reflect on them in whatever historical study they undertake: 'how do we know' is as important an historical question as 'what do we know'.

How much of Pepys's diary is fact and how much is fiction? Can we ever know? Is the question worth asking? The answer must always be 'yes', not because we can ever know such a thing, but because children need to be aware, from a very young age, that historians combine evidence with imagination in their reconstructions of the historical past and that historical stories are subtle amalgamations of both. It is only when they are aware of this that they will be able to make distinctions between factual and fictional representations. This has implications not only for their study of history but also for their perceptions of reality, as Bruner (1986, 1996) argues, our understanding and knowledge of the world is constructed from the stories we tell and the stories we have told to us. The process of distinguishing truth from fiction in stories is not solely a skill children should learn in school for the purposes of understanding history, but is part of a critical mode of thinking that people need to develop throughout their whole lives.

## Useful further reading

*Narrative Matters: Teaching and Learning History through Story*, G. Bage (1999). Bristol: Falmer Press.

Perhaps the definitive work on the use of historical narrative in teaching. A personal and scholarly examination of the subject.

*The Culture of Education*, J. Bruner (1996). Cambridge, Mass.: Harvard University Press.

A difficult read but within its pages is an original explanation of the relationship between thinking, feeling and culture. Chapter 7 is particularly relevant to understanding history.

*Using Semi-Structured Interviews in Small-Scale Research*: A Teacher's Guide, E. Drever (1995). Edinburgh: Scottish Council for Research in Education.

A most useful little handbook for those wishing to carry out classroom research. Suitable for the beginner and the more experienced.

*Teaching as Storytelling: An Alternative Approach to Teaching and the Curriculum*, K. Egan (1988). London: Routledge.

An interesting book for those looking to take an unconventional approach to their teaching. Egan has the nasty habit of being proved right in the long run!

*What is History Teaching? Language, Ideas and Meaning in Learning about the Past*, C. Husbands (1996). Buckingham: Open University Press.

Still the best book for teachers of history at whatever age. Designed for secondary school teachers it has a relevance for all – a well I frequently dip into!

## References

Bage, G. (1999) *Narrative Matters: Teaching and Learning History through Story*. Bristol: Falmer Press.

Bruner, J. (1986) *Actual Minds, Possible Worlds*. Cambridge, Mass.: Harvard University Press.

Bruner, J. (1996) *The Culture of Education*, Cambridge, Mass.: Harvard University Press.

Claire, H.. (1996) *Reclaiming our Pasts, Equality and Diversity in the Primary History Curriculum*. Stoke-on-Trent: Trentham Books.

Department for Education (DfE) (1995) *Key Stages 1 and 2 of the National Curriculum*. London: HMSO.

Department for Education and Employment (DfEE) (1998) A *Scheme of Work for Key Stages One and Two*. London: QCA.

Department of Education and Science (DES) (1991) *History and the National Curriculum*. London: HMSO.

Drever, E. (1995) *Using Semi-Structured Interviews in Small-Scale Research. A Teacher's Guide*. Edinburgh: Scottish Council for Research in Education.

Egan, K. (1986) *Individual Development and the Curriculum*. London: Hutchinson.

Egan, K. (1988) *Teaching as Storytelling. An Alternative Approach to Teaching and the Curriculum*. London: Routledge.

Hoodless, P. (1998) *History and English in the Primary School*. London: Routledge.

Husbands, C. (1996) *What is History Teaching? Language Ideas and Meaning in Learning about the Past*. Buckingham: Open University Press.

National Curriculum Council (NCC) (1993) *Teaching History at Key Stage One*. London: NCC INSET Resources.

Schools Examination and Assessment Council (SEAC) (1993) *Standard Assessment Tasks for History in Key Stage One*. London: SEAC.

Scott, D., and Usher, R. (1999)*Researching Education. Data Methods and Theory in Educational Enquiry*. London: Cassell.

Vass, P. (1996) *A Survey of Primary Teachers Use of Story in Teaching History,* unpublished.

White, H. (1987)*The Content of the Form*. Baltimore, Md.: Johns Hopkins University Press.

Zemon Davies, N. (1987) *Fiction in the Archives*. Oxford: Polity Press.

**History link resource: Stages of follow-up to story-telling**

1. **Ice-breaking**

   Teacher-led questions to children. Children are asked their opinion of the story based on their feelings towards it.

   - Did you enjoy the story?
   - Which 'bits' did you like best?
   - Why did you enjoy that particularly?, etc.

2. **Important bits**

   Teacher asks the children to decide five or six key events in the story. It is important that this is an individual task and children are choosing events that they deem to be significant.

3. **Framing**

   The children record the events pictorially with, perhaps, an explanatory sentence and place them in a chronological order.

4. **An order of events**

   The children's sequences are shared and discussed.

   - Why did you feel a particular event to be important?
   - Why is it important to you?

   Alternative frames are considered and discussed.

5. **Telling the truth**

   Teacher-led questioning. The questioning of the events within the story now begins.

   - Are there any events within the story that might not be true?
   - Which ones?
   - Why?
   - What makes the events believable or unbelievable?

6. **Recording opinions**

   The children return to their picture frames. Underneath each one they write:

   - 'I think this really happened because _____ ', or
   - 'I think this didn't happen because _____ '

   and give reasons for their answers.

## Chapter 12

# Information and communications technology: investigating new frontiers

*Jonathan Allen*

The focus of this chapter is a case study of word processing at Key Stage 2. Despite the variety of experience presented by information and communications technology (ICT), word processing remains central to most children's use of computers. It therefore follows that an understanding of the dynamics involved in this activity is the key to a teacher's planning and implementation of purposeful work involving ICT. To assist further with planning, a photocopiable list of word processing skills is provided as the link resource for this chapter. The case study also illustrates a more general and urgent need for considered research into ICT in the classroom and it will be argued that the novelty of ICT makes the role of research in fostering good practice even more significant than it might be in other subjects. This prompts further questions not only about ICT itself, but also its impact on, and implications for the rest of the curriculum.

## Introduction

Most of the disciplines covered in this book are associated with a substantial body of research material that has served to underpin work in the classroom. A corpus of understanding has built up through the efforts of successive researchers and practitioners. At the same time, despite all the changes, initiatives and modifications to the curriculum, the primary classroom is still recognisably the place it was a generation ago. The main point of difference both physically and in terms of the curriculum is likely to be the presence of ICT – which precisely because of its relatively recent introduction to the curriculum has no comparable theoretical heritage. In terms of delivery, teachers are endeavouring to integrate ICT appropriately into their subject teaching as well as transferring to children the competence to become effective users of the new technologies. Many teachers have largely had to find their own way to manage a constructive accommodation of ICT, seeking support from colleagues, friends and other agencies as the occasion arises. It is only through the recently announced New Opportunities Fund (NOF) initiative that a concerted attempt is being made to tackle nationally the need to develop the technical and pedagogical skills of the profession as a whole in this field. At the time of writing, the success of this project, which will take several years to complete, has still to be assessed.

One of the requirements under the NOF initiative, paralleled in teacher training by DfEE Circular 4/98, is that practitioners should know 'about current classroom-focused research and inspection evidence about the application of ICT to teaching their specialist subject(s), and where it can be found' (DfEE 1998: 31, 1999: 12). The purpose of this chapter is to exemplify supportive research. A case study of word processing in Key Stage 2 will show how a studied analysis of classroom activity should prompt at least significant reflection on practice. It is also anticipated that this might provide the starting point for revision of a teacher's own understanding, and hence planning and implementation of children's learning.

## Can research keep up?

Let us place our commentary in context. The relative novelty of ICT – after all, it only received the status of a discrete subject in the National Curriculum as recently as 1995 – to some extent sets it apart from other subjects. The speed with which ICT is developing has presented a succession of exciting opportunities for education. Many of the ICT resources now available in the classroom – multimedia applications, scanners, digital cameras and much else – have only had significant uptake by schools over the past few years. Even the World Wide Web, now so central to computer usage, was introduced on the Internet in 1991, and has been only widely taken up by schools much more recently. Those who have witnessed the development of ICT in education over the past decade, whether as practitioners or researchers, will recognise that the activities now taking place in many classrooms represent a huge evolution over what previously was possible. This process will continue. The nascent National Grid for Learning has the potential to revolutionise teaching and learning as we now understand it (Ager 1998: 21). Yet the shallow lineage of ICT in no sense negates the need for research evidence on which to build good practice. Indeed, since many teachers would freely admit their relative lack of expertise in this area (Somekh and Davis 1997: 115; Smith 1999: 2), the support that research can provide becomes all the more critical.

If ICT has only a short history, it is an unusually dynamic one. This means that there is no large cadre of precedents for the subject that can yet provide a comprehensive theoretical framework in education. Likewise, maxims of the 'We've always done it this way' variety, always worth questioning, are untenable in the context of the subject. The recent debate over the change of name from Information Technology (IT) to Information and Communications Technology if nothing else reflects pedagogic uncertainty. The educational arena in this country is replacing the conventional 'IT', standard nomenclature for the new technologies in other spheres of activity, with 'ICT', an abbreviation largely unfamiliar to the rest of the world. It remains to be seen whether education represents the vanguard, or rather is shifting tangentially in a direction which will not appeal to others.

In consequence of this state of flux it is arguable that research dating from only a few years ago will have questionable relevance in today's classroom. Certainly there is a difficulty with investigations into the use of specific software packages which have now been superseded. By the same token, any report about, for example, the use of the World Wide Web in schools will by definition be recent. Nevertheless, treated with due circumspection, older material still has a resonance. For example, *Mindstorms*, in which Seymour Papert (1993) discusses the development of LOGO, remains a seminal work, more powerful, probably, than his more recent *The Children's Machine* (Papert 1994).

It is also worth bearing in mind a distinction between research and publications that may be broadly summarised as hints and tips. The latter may be very valuable (for example Bennett 1997; Higgins *et al.* 1999), but they serve a different purpose. They tend to be catalogues of bright ideas and technical expositions rather than explorations of why and how ICT works with children. As Moira Monteith has put it, 'the use and implementation of ICT in learning needs to be carefully contextualised with due note taken of research findings and good practice where learning gains have been substantiated' (Monteith 1998: 3).

## Children writing words and building thoughts

The research selected for discussion in this chapter will elucidate this distinction. John Jessel introduces his research by reminding us of the important role of text in thinking and learning (Jessel 1997). Through text we are able to take our thoughts and crystallise them on paper. We can consider what we have written, read it again, develop our notions, revise what we have written and ultimately move on to new ideas. Jessel sees this process in part as a way of 'unburdening the memory' (Jessel 1997: 28), clearing it out to provide a *tabula rasa* for new ideas. And, of course, these activities serve to make public our conceptions. Text is a powerful means of disseminating and sharing what has happened in our mind.

Text has always had this capacity to mediate thought. However, Jessel continues by noting that word processing presents children (and no doubt adults too) with a flexibility that traditional materials – most obviously paper and pencil – cannot match. The contrast is distilled in what Jessel terms the 'non-permanence' of electronic media. Children may use an eraser to correct or improve what they have written on paper, but the ease with which changes may be effected using a word processor is of a different order.

The postulations here are not new. Intuitively, any adult user of a word processor will understand the distinction that is being made, and Jessel cites a number of writers who, recognising the potential of the word processor to facilitate the redrafting of text, have championed its use in children's writing. Yet there is a difficulty. The logic that suggests that word processing self-evidently represents a more effective way for children to create texts is not reflected by recorded observation. The opportunity is clearly there, but it is not necessarily realised in practice.

Jessel, based at Goldsmith's College, University of London, determined to examine this conundrum more closely through research into the use of word processing by nine- and ten-year-old children in a South London primary school. The research is essentially qualitative in nature, Jessel closely monitoring the process taking place as the children undertook work on the computer. Although there is no description of a systematic action research model being used, it is evident that Jessel had the opportunity for 'participant observation' (Blease and Cohen 1990), which enabled him to initiate the work and also intervene in an attempt to steer the children along particular avenues.

The children were given tasks – story writing – that offered plenty of opportunities for redrafting. The theme of their story was agreed, and in some cases a sentence by which the story would end was negotiated, the intention being to encourage the young authors to project and plan their ideas with a conclusion in mind. Additionally, arrangements were made for the children to work in pairs so that discussion might stimulate both the development and the revision of material.

Jessel reviews the work and interactions of pairs of children, and also the activity of children who were working independently, in some detail. As an aside, it is worth considering in general the wealth of data that a researcher can draw from a short period's work on the computer by a pair of children (the analyses of Wegerif and Scrimshaw (1997) and Mercer and Wegerif (1999) provide a different, but equally fascinating, perspective). Certainly the minutiae of what takes place would, of necessity, regularly escape teachers as they deal with the whole class. What emerges from Jessel's observations, though, is quite stark and readily summarised. The children's writing was not reflective in the sense of demonstrating a spontaneous consideration of what they had written with a view to possible modification. Some modification of syntax took place, but redrafting was minimal and typically the result of adult prompting. Nor did the children engage in any substantive exchanges furthering the development of their ideas for the story line.

While the pattern characterising the children's computer use is easy to discern, explaining it is more complex. Jessel starts by examining the origin of stories, using the model developed by Bereiter and Scardamalia (1987). The process is represented in three stages. Ideas are 'accessed', then content is 'selected' with the selection subsequently being 'encoded' into writing. Jessel suggests that what is taking place here may well not be manifest, particularly at the starting point, before anything has been written. It may be very difficult to express the essence of the plot or the story line in a few words. If this is accepted, then expectations of children collaborating are optimistic. Even after writing has begun, higher order skills are demanded not only to recognise weaknesses but also to act constructively to improve on them. To make the further demand of compromise with a co-worker is a requirement that several of the children expressly felt that they could do without. For example, Sam is quoted as saying, 'You have more ideas if you work on your own, the other person puts you off' (Jessel 1997: 33).

Jessel continues by debating whether any practical obstacles might be inhibiting children in the redrafting of their texts. The obvious possibility that the children did not have sufficient word processing competence is considered by the researcher as unlikely to apply in the particular case studies. More subtly, however, Jessel points out that there is a sense in which making an amendment in a word processing document has a connotation of finality; changing something may mean losing it. Also significantly, Jessel notes that redrafting as a continuous process on the computer diverges from the conventional approach with which the children would be familiar whereby a first draft is handwritten, reviewed by the teacher and then reworked as a fair copy. Apart from the organisational differences, that latter arrangement anyhow does not lend itself to a major review of the material that has been produced. We will return to this point shortly.

The conclusions that Jessel derives from his research are important:

- Neither discussion nor redrafting appear to be automatic outcomes of the use by children of word processing. It is suggested, rather, that, 'If children do have the intellectual apparatus to allow reflection and revision in their thinking, then it is possible that a number of techniques could be developed to encourage this process' (Jessel 1997: 35).
- The role of the teacher in supporting children in the development of their capability for redrafting is seen as critical. Jessel refines this argument to the point of advocating that language curriculum specialists need to be involved here, rather than placing reliance on operational skills taught by a computer specialist (Jessel 1997: 36) – a slightly curious distinction in an article that is mainly about primary practice, but the underlying point is valid.
- An intriguing contrast is made between the quality of the ideas and the surface detail of writing. For both the child and the adult, meaning is much more difficult to assess than aspects of writing such as spelling and punctuation. In consequence the latter aspects may well receive undue precedence, especially if the finished effort is to be displayed or otherwise subjected to general scrutiny. This emphasis is likely to be reinforced by the rough draft to fair copy approach to which we alluded earlier.

If redrafting presents such a difficult challenge in the classroom, then it is reasonable to ask whether the dedication of so much computer time to word processing is appropriate. Jessel notes facility with presentation and being able to make minor alterations quickly as reasons enough to continue, and few would dispute these advantages. However he goes on to stress that we should not expect that in their use of word processing children are following the same agenda as professional writers. Children may well be thinking of their story as something to be completed by playtime, rather than as their life's work. What is being required of the reader, ultimately, is to evaluate the way in which word processing is implemented only within the context of the way that words and writing are already managed in the classroom as a whole.

## Taking the debate further

Jessel's paper is stimulating and thought provoking and prompts responses in a variety of directions. Let us, though, return to the main thread. Despite the potential that may be obvious to adult writers, children appear not to exploit the opportunity for redrafting that word processing presents. This may be, quite simply, because the children have not been taught to do it. In demonstrating that word processing is different both technically and intellectually from using a paper and pencil to write, the logic must follow that just as we support children in their development of traditional approaches to writing so we must consider how the new medium for expression, word processing, should be taught.

Some illustrations will elaborate this point. Certain aspects of word processing are fundamental and will be learned at a functional level. Without understanding them it will be almost impossible to create anything. Simple examples would include using the shift key to obtain capital letters, or understanding that the backspace key removes the previous character. Children will learn these techniques by asking friends or their teacher, as they need to know them in order to make any progress. However, a more sophisticated skill would be the use of a centring button or menu command to centre text. There are other ways, such as employing the space bar, or tab key, of moving text centrally, and novice users may quickly apply these. The centring tool, though, has the advantage of allowing subsequent adjustments to the font. Text will remain centred despite any changes to its size. This feature may not be apparent and may well need to be taught to a user – whatever their age.

It is presumably to techniques such as these that Jessel refers when he notes that 'A further reason why revisions were not frequent is that the children observed may have considered that they were not sufficiently adept at using the word processor, or that their typing skills were lacking'. He concludes that this was probably not the problem, but suggests that 'it is one thing to be aware of the existence of editing facilities and quite another to use them when the occasion requires it' (Jessel 1997: 34). This is critical. The understanding of how valuable the redrafting capability of a word processor might be is not intuitive; it needs to be taught.

Redrafting is not simply a mechanical process. Certainly it requires the technical under-standing of how the text can be manipulated (cutting, copying and pasting, for example), but the insight into recognising the potential of these processes is of a different order. Just as it is proposed that many technical skills will need to be taught, so it is essential that children should be carefully supported in their developing understanding of what the computer will enable them to do. (McFarlane (1997: 114–15) elaborates this argument.) It is easy to recognise why children resist redrafting when using a paper and pencil. It is extremely time consuming. We would not expect adults to carry out this sort of work (although when talking to higher education students about their assignments, it appears that many do). The nature of the same task using a word processor is entirely different. The author can afford to experiment, write in note form, and pay attention asynchro-nously to matters of content, style, syntax, spelling and punctuation. All this is possible because redrafting on the computer is so quick and easy. It does, though, require of both the teacher and the taught a radical departure in the way that the writing of texts is approached. The computer must not be seen as simply a means for presenting a fair copy; it represents, rather, a comprehensive alternative channel through which texts may be developed from conception to completion.

## Handwriting and word processing: balancing a question?

Let us live dangerously and push this argument a bit further. Opportunities to 'assemble and develop ideas on paper and on screen' are firmly embedded in the recently revised National Curriculum requirements for English (DfEE/QCA 1999) (a similar require-ment was also found in DFE (1995)). The skills involved are, it may be assumed, hand-writing techniques on the one hand and word processing on the other. In the same docu-ment, the Key Stage programmes of study make detailed reference to the development of handwriting skills. This is reinforced by the attainment targets, in which the levels make specific reference to handwriting. An interesting hypothesis about how word processing might, in practice, support the development of handwriting is found in Crompton and Mann (1996: 34). However, the new National Curriculum changes the emphasis significantly: 'To overcome any potential barriers to learning in English, some pupils may require . . . opportunities to learn and develop alternative methods of recording, such as ICT, to compensate for difficulties with handwriting, to enable them to demonstrate their wider writing skills' (DfEE/QCA 1999).

This is quite contrary to our experience as adults. In the workplace there is now an expectation that written material will be presented in word processed form, especially if the document is of any length, or in any sense formal. For many, even those who attended school in a pre-computer age and so only experienced there the 'on-paper' option for redrafting (or, more likely, managed to avoid redrafting altogether), the advantages of the word processor in this respect are anyhow too beguiling. 'Personal' correspondence (and of course email) is now frequently typed. Teaching may well be the last occupation that makes substantial use of handwriting, and the introduction of new technologies into the classroom will undermine even this bastion (but see Griffin (1995: 3–4) for anecdotes of how slow the process may be). For much of the rest of the population the application of handwriting has been reduced to signatures, form filling and shopping lists.

The argument here is not that developing children's handwriting is a waste of time. There are clear benefits in the development of motor control and – for those who *do* manage to develop attractive calligraphy – possibly in self-esteem. There is, also, evidence that where handwriting and spelling are taught together children's spelling benefits (see Mudd 1994: 89). Furthermore it is unlikely that handwriting's utility will be completely eroded. Yet it is undeniable that handwriting is not used as much as it was formerly. However, unlike word processing, it remains a central skill in the English curriculum. The relative positioning might productively be questioned.

If these comments seem radical, at one level all they reduce to is a plea for word processing in schools to be given the attention it deserves so that its benefits and advantages may be exploited. Children (and adult learners) may discover a tremendous amount about an application simply by having the time to explore it. They will determine how to make things work, create certain effects, either serendipitously or by trial and error. However, it is not enough simply to let children loose on the computer without support. Capability with word processing has become too important a life skill to leave its acquisition to chance.

There is, though, a more fundamental point which the juxtaposing of handwriting and word processing serves to illustrate. The impact of the new technologies, and other societal changes too, is such that we must question, and if necessary overhaul, the curriculum that we have inherited. Do we have the right priorities? Are we teaching children what they need to know, or what we needed to know?

## Link resource

This activity is intended to provide a planning tool for the development of English and ICT schemes of work. It only takes a short time to complete, but in focusing attention on the need to ensure that children's appropriation of word processing skills is systematic, it supports the underlying argument that their understanding should not be left to chance. It needs to be planned, guided and nurtured.

*Context*
An individual teacher, perhaps the ICT coordinator, might undertake the exercise, but it is better suited to discussion among a small group of teachers during a planning meeting.

*Process*
1. Photocopy the resource page (page 139) on to card and cut out the rectangles indicated.
2. Arrange the skills into a sequence that is considered to provide logical progression.
3. Sub-divide the skills into the years when they might be taught.
4. Classify the skills into those which are straightforward *technical* processes and those which make *intellectual* demands on the user (they represent new ways of thinking about the learner's work).

*Outcomes*
At a practical level, the exercise should provide helpful input into the school's scheme of work. There is no correct order. Especially for a Key Stage 1 team, some of the skills will not be appropriate for the age phase (some might even be better left until Key Stage 3, but they should be considered nevertheless). QCA (1998) provides helpful guidance in the preparation of ICT schemes of work.

Equally important is the debate itself. The thought and discussion that the activity will prompt should draw attention not just to progression in the development of word processing skills, but to the importance of delivering these in a concerted way.

## Conclusions

Through the planned NOF expenditure amounting to £230 million the government has given a clear signal of the importance that is attached to the teaching of ICT in our schools. The initiative also reflects the considerable need to develop the competence of so many teachers in this area. Although disconcerting in terms of the national picture for ICT in education, teachers may perhaps take heart from the implication that if they view the subject with a degree of circumspection they are not alone.

There is no escaping the fact that the task ahead is considerable. First there is the necessity of gaining technical competence. Understanding ICT at the level at which we use it in school may not be too difficult a challenge intellectually but it makes substantial demands on time for those starting from a low baseline. Additionally, beyond developing their technical expertise, teachers need also to devise strategies for the useful and effective implementation of ICT in their lesson planning. There needs to be recognition, too, that ICT in the classroom will not just happen; it needs to be planned and taught. Research and the experience of other practitioners have plenty to offer in this respect, supplementing what for many teachers may be a thin layer of existing personal experience.

There will be a further stage in the development of ICT in schools, however. Whether we like it or not, ICT is subverting established perceptions of how the world works. As teachers we cannot regard it simply as a tool, albeit a powerful one (DfEE 1999). We need to consider instead, as in our example of word processing's impact on the importance of handwriting, how ICT will come to modify, rather than just support, the existing curriculum.

## Useful further reading

*The Role of IT: Practical Issues for the Primary Teacher*, A. Loveless (1998). London: Cassell Academic.

This book takes further the discussion of the part that ICT plays in relation to the rest of the curriculum, examining its contribution from a variety of viewpoints.

*100 Ideas for IT*, G. Smith (1998). London: Collins Educational.

As an additional useful example of reference sources that are available to support the effective use of ICT in the classroom this book complements the research-based analysis that was the focus of this chapter.

*Life on the Screen: Identity in the Age of the Internet*, S. Turkle (1996). London: Weidenfeld and Nicholson.

Although there is only passing reference to children's use of computers, *Life on the Screen* is recommended to prompt reflection on the wider impact that new technologies are having on Western society.

## References

Ager, R. (1998) *Information and Communications Technology in Primary Schools: Children or Computers in Control?* London: David Fulton Publishers.

Bennett, R. (1997) *Teaching at Key Stage 1: Teaching IT*. Oxford: Nash Pollock Publishing.

Bereiter, C. and Scardamalia, M. (1987) *The Psychology of Composition*. Hillsdale, N.J.: Lawrence Erlbaum Associates.

Blease, D. and Cohen, L. (1990) *Coping with Computers: An Ethnographic Study of the Primary Classroom*. London: Paul Chapman Publishing.

Crompton, R. and Mann, P. (1996) 'Communicating information: words', in Crompton, R. and Mann, P. (eds) *IT Across the Primary School Curriculum*. London: Cassell.

Department for Education (DfE) (1995) *Key Stages 1 and 2 of the National Curriculum*. London: HMSO Publications Centre.

Department for Education and Employment (DfEE) (1998) *Teaching: High Status, High Standards – Requirements for Courses of Initial Teacher Training* (Circular 4/98). London: DfEE.

Department for Education and Employment (DfEE) (1999) *The Use of ICT in Subject Teaching: Expected Outcomes for Teachers in England, Wales and Northern Ireland*. London: TTA.

DfEE/QCA (1999) *The National Curriculum for England: English*. London: DfEE/QCA available from the WWW, http://www.nc.uk.net (accessed 23 November 1999).

Griffin, J (1995) 'Introduction', in Griffin, J. and Bash, L. (eds) *Computers in the Primary School*. London: Cassell.

Higgins, S. *et al.* (1999) *500 ICT Tips for Primary Teachers*. London: Kogan Page.

Jessel, J. (1997) 'Writing words and building thoughts', in Somekh, B. and Davis, N. (eds) *Using Information Technology Effectively in Teaching and Learning: Studies in Pre-service and In-service Teacher Education*. London: Routledge.

McFarlane, A. (1997) 'Thinking about writing', in McFarlane, A. (ed.) *Information Technology and Authentic Learning*. London: Routledge.

Mercer, N. and Wegerif, R. (1999) 'Is "exploratory talk" productive talk?', in Littleton, K. and Light, P. (eds) *Learning With Computers: Analysing Productive Interaction*. London: Routledge.

Monteith, M. (1998) 'Introduction', in Monteith, M. (ed.) *IT for Learning Enhancement*. Exeter: Intellect Books.

Mudd, N. (1994) *Effective Spelling*. London: Hodder & Stoughton.

Papert, S. (1993) *Mindstorms: Children, Computers and Powerful Ideas,* 2nd edn (1st edn 1980). Hemel Hempstead: Harvester Wheatsheaf.

Papert, S. (1994) *The Children's Machine: Rethinking School in the Age of the Computer*. Hemel Hempstead: Harvester Wheatsheaf.

Smith, H. (1999) *Opportunities for Information and Communication Technology in the Primary School*. Stoke on Trent: Trentham Books Limited.

Somekh, B. and Davis, N. (1997) 'Getting teachers started with IT and transferable skills', in Somekh, B. and Davis, N. (eds) *Using Information Technology Effectively in Teaching and Learning: Studies in Pre-service and In-service Teacher Education*. London: Routledge.

Qualifications and Curriculum Authority (QCA) (1998) *A Scheme of Work for Key Stages 1 and 2: Information Technology*. London: QCA.

Wegerif, R. and Scrimshaw, P. (1997) *Computers and Talk in the Primary Classroom*. Clevedon: Multilingual Matters Ltd.

# ICT link resource: Planning to develop children's word processing skills

| | |
|---|---|
| Use shift key to create capitals | Adjust margins |
| Print work | Use a spell checker |
| Edit text by using arrow keys/mouse | Use a grammar checker |
| Save work | Change font size |
| Insert a graphic (e.g. clip art) | Move and resize a graphic (e.g. clip art) |
| Use frames | Use backspace key |
| Create a table | Change page layout: portrait/landscape |
| Use enter/return key | Align text (left, right, centre or fully justified) |
| Delete text | Change font colour |
| Adjust paper size | Enter text to create words |
| Use punctuation | Create a border |
| Use find and replace | Use space bar |
| Choose text style: bold/italic/underline | Start a new document |
| Use zoom | Use the mouse to position the cursor |
| Edit text by cut/copy and paste | Highlight text |
| Load an existing document | Use a word bank to create simple sentences |

# Chapter 13

# Motivating the musically disaffected

*Mary Kellett*

This chapter discusses a research project exploring musical listening skills with a class of six- to nine-year-olds, spanning Key Stages 1 and 2. Completely new activities were designed so that the disaffected and less musically able would not feel disadvantaged. The 'expert status' of all children was constantly reinforced. A non-threatening environment was created by the reassurance that there were no right or wrong answers, and non-verbal stimuli were used to scaffold responses. The results showed that listening skills developed significantly and musical self-esteem was raised. The greatest measurable progress was made by the less able and those with low self-esteem. Implications for teaching and issues of balance between the three components of the music curriculum are also discussed. A photocopiable link resource including suggestions of how the activities might be used in the classroom is provided.

## Introduction

Children frequently equate musicality with the ability to sing well or play an instrument. Sadly, this association often leads to low musical self-esteem in those children who regard themselves as having neither a singing nor instrumental skill. The emphasis on perform-ance-based activities in many primary schools can unwittingly reinforce this perception, accelerating the downward spirals of low achievement and low self-esteem which lead to disaffection. The research project described in this chapter offers an opportunity to reverse this trend. It focuses on the listening component of the music curriculum. Listen-ing tends to be a less threatening activity than performing and need not be viewed as passive; indeed, it is an active, perceptual experience requiring sustained concentration.

## Recent research into children's musical listening responses

With the exception of music preference, there has been little research based around young children's responses to music (Kratus 1993). Most of the studies with young children used the judgements of professional adult musicians to norm reference the child response rather than exploring the child response for its own intrinsic value. Terwogt and Van Grinsven (1991) explored musical expression of mood states with groups of five-year-olds, ten-year-olds and adults. Extracts of music were linked to four prescribed mood states: happiness, sadness, fear and anger. They found a considerable consensus of choice in the groups and that this correlation increased with age. However, their research also highlighted difficulties children experienced in trying to justify their experiences verbally. Other researchers like Kastner and Crowder (1990) and Dolgin and Adelson (1990) have used schematic facial expressions to make choice definition more accessible to children.

Kratus's large study (1993) involving 658 children aged six to twelve years explored differences in children's ability to interpret emotion in music by requiring them to circle happy, sad, excited or calm faces as they listened to music. The musical extracts were varied for texture, dynamics, harmony, melody and rhythm, but style and performing medium were kept constant. He found a high incidence of agreement unaffected by gender and age bands, concluding that emotional interpretation of music was not significantly affected by formal musical training. Giomo (1993) worked with two groups of children aged five and nine and used 49 schematic cartoons to elicit responses. Unlike Terwogt and van Grinsven (1991) and Dolgin and Adelson (1990), whose studies showed increased correlation the higher the age group, Giomo found an insignificant difference and concluded that the use of non-verbal stimuli was enabling younger children to perform at a higher level.

Swanwick and Tillman's (1986) substantial research defined stages of musical development at different ages in their 'developmental spiral'. It began with very young children at a sensory/manipulative level in the 'material' part of the spiral, moving towards personal/vernacular skills in the 'expressive' section, developing further into the speculative/idiomatic in the 'form' part of the spiral and finally, at the teenage years, to higher order symbolic/systematic skills in the 'value' section. Hentschke's (1993) work on children's response to music used illustrations of stick people in various poses of activity as a stimulus. She claimed that the relationship between intuitive response and analysis was mutually reinforcing and something that could be actively developed in children.

Ward (1986) was one of the few researchers to value the child perspective without reference to adult norms. Basing his work on Kelly's (1955) theory of personal constructs he measured musical response in seven-year-olds. Using an 'odd one out' strategy he enabled children to form constructs such as consonance and dissonance without necessarily having the verbal skills to explain this. Gilbert (1990) also acknowledged that the constraint of verbal responses impeded a true reflection of the way in which music was being construed.

These recent studies have undoubtedly contributed to a better understanding of children's response to music. However, as far as can be determined, most of them rely on adult norms and the linking of developmental trends to age and musical experience. There appears to be a shortage of child-centred research, undertaken in real-world environments, exploring and valuing children's musical responses for their own sake, referenced to neither adult criteria nor the constraints of verbal competence. The following project attempts to redress this imbalance.

## The research project

This action research was undertaken as part of a Master's degree. It took place in a village school with a mixed-age class of six- to nine-year-olds and was incorporated into the normal teaching week. The two outcomes sought were:

- a better understanding of children's listening responses; and
- an answer to the hypothesis that intervention activities could lead to a *development* in children's listening skills.

In pursuit of these outcomes, the most appropriate methodology was judged to be one encompassing aspects of quasi-experimental action research within an overall case study.

### Measuring the intervention

In order to have some initial baseline from which to compare developments, a simple self-assessment, adapted from Salmon (1995), was introduced. This sought to establish an initial measurement of self-perceived musicality. This same assessment was used again at the end of the project to discover whether children's self-perception changed. The children placed a mark on a line to indicate their self-perceived musicality: 'where I think I am on this line'.

not musical _____ very musical

Another line was marked to show their perception of how they thought their peers viewed their musicality: 'where I think my friends would put me on this line'. A second pair of lines was used to measure their self-perception of their musical listening skills and their perception of how their peers viewed their listening skills.

### The action research

The class was divided into groups of eight and the teacher worked with each group for half an hour exclusively. Every child was given their own set of colours, patterns (computer generated) and textures (bubble wrap, cotton wool, velvet, suede leather, shiny paper, chiffon, sacking and sandpaper). On a weekly basis, spanning a complete term, children listened to a one-minute extract of music. The extracts covered a wide range – solo, ensemble, orchestral – and were taken from Western and non-Western styles. A discography appears in the link resource on page 148.

As they listened, children made a choice from one of the sets of stimuli which they judged best matched the music. Afterwards, they were encouraged to discuss reasons for their choices. The teacher went to great lengths to persuade them they were all experts, and that their choices were equally valued. It was hoped, firstly, that giving children a metaphorical 'expert hat' would lead to better performance and raised musical self-esteem. Secondly, it would determine whether using non-verbal tasks could help overcome some language communication problems. In the early weeks there were a few occasions of children wanting to choose the same as their best friend, but they soon developed enough confidence to make their own decisions and to justify them in the plenary. In the first three weeks only the colours and pattern sheets were used. Initially these were given to the children separately so that they only had to think about one type of choice, but as they became increasingly familiar with the format both sheets were introduced for one musical extract. The textures were introduced at Week 4.

## Validity

There were several threats to the validity of this project. Because I was both class teacher and participant researcher, children might have sought to 'please' in their responses by saying and choosing what they thought I wanted to hear. Measures were taken to counter-act this, particularly in choice of spoken word and body language which might inadvert-ently lead their responses. The positive stance about them being experts and there being no right or wrong answer helped to minimise any likelihood of 'teacher pleasing'. In addition, all sessions were videotaped and the tapes made available for independent observer checks. Meticulous analysis of the tapes also detected whether children were being influenced by peer pressure, friendships or gender. A few instances were noted, but only in the early stages, and as confidence and self-esteem grew, children increasingly valued their own opinions. Sessions were held at exactly the same time of day on the same day of the week to reduce affective physical bias such as children being more tired at one session than another, particularly as the activity relied on concentration and listening. Triangulation of data – observation notes, pre- and post-test self-assessments and individual interviews – was adopted (Nisbett and Watt 1987) to minimise any possible researcher observation bias.

## Findings

The findings from the project are divided into two sections: those that derived from analysis of my observations; and those that derived from the pre- and post-test self-assessments.

### Researcher observations

Prior to the project, comments from listening to music in other lessons had been based on emotional response to the music; for example *it's sad* or *it's nice*. However, once we started using the pattern choice activities and the 'expert hat' a development in listening skills became noticeable. Comments and observations became more sophisticated and began to focus on technical aspects of the music such as structure, tempo and texture:

> 'I chose this one because there's the same spaces between the dots and it keeps to the same spaces and the music sort of kept to the same beat all the time like if you're walking you're always walking at the same speed.'

> 'I chose this because there are different patterns in it but also they repeat and there were lots of different little patterns in the music that kept repeating.'

> 'I chose this one because it felt like different instruments were coming in and out of the music at different times.'

Children used the visual imagery in a scaffolding process to help identify and interpret what their language skills alone could not communicate, enabling them to share opinions and emotions they had previously found difficult. This was encapsulated by one seven-year-old who said, 'It's sometimes hard to find the words for what you're thinking but the patterns give you ideas and help you think of the words'.

Some subtle changes in group dynamics were observed. The more able, articulate children did not dominate discussions in a way that had been noticeable in other class lessons. Children who were normally reluctant to share their opinions for fear of being sneered at, became increasingly confident about sharing their thoughts. In particular, musically disaffected children with low self-esteem who resisted participating in performance activities for fear of ridicule became eager to demonstrate their listening skills.

*Self assessments*

Raw scores from the before and after self-assessment measures were converted to percentages for ease of comparison. They were analysed in two ways:

- overall averages for the whole class; and
- differentials for each individual child.

Class averages are shown in Table 13.1 and an example of differential scores from an individual case study are shown in Figure 13.1.

**Table 13.1 Overall class averages (percentages)**

| Assessment | Before | After | Increase |
|---|---|---|---|
| Self – musicality | 60.01 | 65.60 | 5.50 |
| Self – listening | 67.40 | 71.90 | 4.50 |
| Peer – musicality | 58.30 | 59.70 | 1.40 |
| Peer – listening | 52.70 | 63.00 | 10.30 |

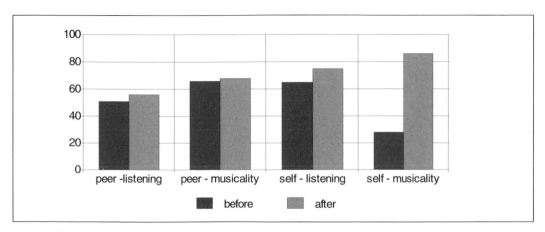

**Figure 13.1** Example of an individual child's differentials

Obviously the findings cannot be generalised more widely since a single class is an extremely small and unrepresentative sample. However, the data are significant enough to show trends and prompt some areas of discussion. The overwhelming majority of children showed an increase in all four self-assessed categories and I was encouraged by the high level of concentration and sophisticated listening skills that were being unconsciously developed.

It is impossible to report on the outcomes for all the children (see Kellett (1998) for more detailed analysis) but some individual cases do warrant special mention, in particular one eight-year-old boy who was registered as having special educational needs. He was small for his age, slight of stature and suffered from a disfiguring eczema condition which other children responded unkindly to. His pre-intervention self-assessment with regard to where he thought his peers might place him on the musical listening skills line was heartbreaking. In percentage terms it equated with a woeful 1%. At the end of the project this had increased to 48%; modest in comparison to some of the more confident children in the class, but it represented a giant step for him. On one occasion, he delivered this comment confidently in front of the whole group,

> 'I chose this one (a pattern) because it (the music) sounded like flashing lights and fountains. I could see fountains shooting up into the air, different coloured fountains, lots of different coloured water like you see in those shows at Alton Towers and stuff. The pattern looked like the fountains shooting up and down. I liked this music.'

From a boy with language special needs these comments were quite a revelation. In addition to the improvement in his perception of how his peers ranked him, his musical listening skills and concentration span, hitherto almost non-existent, were observed to develop dramatically. When I interviewed him at the end of the project, his comments demonstrated this:

> Teacher: Your marks on these lines suggest that you think you're better at listening to music than you were in September. Why do you think that is?
>
> Child: I'm better at listening because I'm good at choosing things that fit the music.
>
> Teacher: How do you feel about yourself and music now?
>
> Child: I think I've got better at music.

Similar developments happened with a nine-year-old boy also registered as having special educational needs. Historically he had a negative attitude towards music, especially if it involved singing, which he described as 'boring and a waste of space'. However, he responded very positively to the listening activities, attaching great importance to the task of making choices that were genuinely valued and made interesting contributions to the discussions. His post-project self-assessment showed improvements in all four categories, and his perception of his musicality rose from 28% to 86%. Comments from his post-project interview were also encouragingly positive:

Teacher: How do you feel about yourself and music?

Child: I think I've got better at music. It's been fun choosing all the patterns and stuff. I think I'm good at that. I used to think I was rubbish at music 'cause I'm rubbish at singing and all that but I think I'm good at doing the patterns and stuff . . . Having to match the colours made me listen harder to the music. I prob'ly heard more things 'cause in some of the pieces there are a lot of things going on at the same time and if I just listened to it without having to choose something I might not hear them.

## Implications for teaching

There are several implications for teaching. These have been organised into four areas: assessment, self-esteem, classroom management and special educational needs.

### *Assessment*

Children's responses to music are often underestimated because of poor concentration span rather than lack of musicality and much potential goes undetected. Young children only communicate a fraction of their response to music because of the limitation of their language skills. This is a disquieting thought when one considers how many judgements and assessments are based on verbal responses.

> Musical perception takes place inside the brain; we cannot tap directly into it. If we want to know if someone is perceiving or not, we have to ask them to sing, speak, write or move, and then measure how well they do that. Any problem may result from difficulty with the singing, speaking, writing or moving itself, rather than the perception.                                  (Mills 1991: 149)

Practitioners are constantly seeking better and more accurate methods to determine children's progress. I believe the activities described in this study could provide a framework for assessment that would not disadvantage children with poor language skills, ensuring that it is actually their musical listening skills which are being assessed.

### *Self-esteem*

There are significant implications with regard to self-esteem. Lawrence (1988) maintains that enhancing self-esteem enhances the child's capacity to cope with learning problems. This research certainly upholds Lawrence's view and adds the dimension that raised self-esteem can also enhance a child's capacity to focus and concentrate. Concentrated listening is a skill required in all areas of education and therefore the findings from this study have potentially wide-reaching implications across the curriculum. 'One of the aims of music education ought to be to develop the ability to listen because it contributes vitally not only to music, but to many other aspects of learning and of life' (Carlton 1987: 11).

## Classroom management

How often have we bemoaned the fact that there are never enough instruments to go round in a music lesson? Everyone wants to play the glockenspiel and nobody wants to be seen dead with a triangle. Composition classes disintegrate into bitter disputes and rivalries over who gets the best instruments. A structured listening skills programme built around the activities described here offers teachers more opportunities to employ group work in music lessons, rotating listening activity groups – using multiple headphones with central tape recorder – with composition/performance groups who would be delighted to have double the choice of instruments.

## Special educational needs

There are extensive implications for the teaching of children with special educational needs. Apart from the progress children made in musical listening, considerable strides were made towards improved language skills, particularly oracy. Effective strategies appear to have been the use of a metaphorical 'expert hat', reduction of anxiety by removing fear of wrong answers, a genuine valuing of the child response and scaffolding (Vygotsky 1962). These are all strategies that are transferable into other curriculum areas.

# Link resource

## Introduction

The listening activities described in this chapter are easily adaptable, and are not onerous to prepare or administer. They can be used for small group work or whole-class teaching. The emphasis on no right or wrong answer and children as the experts means that no specialist music knowledge is required and the non-threatening environment is helpful to those teachers who may be anxious about delivering the music curriculum. The activities also readily lend themselves as projects for non-specialist students working with small groups on school experience. If space is a premium and a quiet area of the classroom is not available, the activities can be conducted using multiple sets of headphones linked to a central tape recorder.

## Suggested discography

The ten musical extracts which follow are those that were used in the research study. They were chosen to reflect a range of periods, multicultural styles and different mixes of instruments and voice. This is only a suggested list and almost any type of music could be used. The length of each extract was one minute and this would seem to be optimum in terms of focused concentration for most primary aged children.

- *Suite Espanola* (solo guitar) by Sanz, 1676
- *Festival Overture* (full orchestra) by Shostakovich, 1957
- *Karibuni* (African tribal song) traditional 20th century

- *Saire Marais* (Royal Marines Brass Band) traditional twentieth-century parade
- *Violin Concerto No. 8* (solo violin with fleeting string echoes) by Louis Spohr, 1823
- *Thep Banthom* (Mahori instrumental ensemble, Thailand) by Ja Pan Payong, 1859
- *Hotta* (synthesiser and acoustic guitar) by Sky, 1979
- *Red in the Rainbow* (American Indian flute music) traditional 19th century
- *Verbum Caro* (a capella choir) by Sheppard, 1553
- *Papalotl* (percussive piano) by Alvarez, 1987

## Getting started – small group work

### Resources
Willing adult; quiet bay of the classroom or separate resource area if available; tape of selected musical extracts (see suggestions in discography); laminated sheets of eight pattern choices (see photocopiable resource) and/or colour choices and/or selection of small samples of different textures (e.g. cotton wool, sandpaper, hessian, velvet, etc.); wipe clean marker pens.

### The activity
It is important to start by reinforcing that there are no right or wrong answers and that everyone's choices and comments are equally valued. Allow the children to listen to the extract a couple of times while concentrating on their pattern/colour sheets, instructing them to tick their best fit choice with the marker pen. Encourage rich discussion regarding reasons for their choices, ensuring everyone in the group gets equal 'air time'.

### Whole-class teaching
If you are not in the fortunate position of having some adult support in your class, it is still possible to use these activities with a whole class. When managing larger numbers like this, it would be advisable to listen to the extract and make individual choices in a whole-class framework, but then divide into groups for discussion with the teacher moving from group to group to motivate, encourage and ensure equal talk opportunities.

### Adaptations
Any number of adaptations could be made to the proposed activities. The musical extracts could have a particular theme rather than being multicultural. Other choice selections could be used such as eight different flowers or plants, different smells, art work or any number of possibilities. Children could be invited to invent their own patterns rather than choosing from prescribed ones.

### Differentiation
These activities could be built into a differentiated scheme of work for the listening component of the curriculum. More able children could be asked to match choices to specific musical elements such as texture, articulation, timbre and form with particular styles of music being chosen to target responses.

## Conclusions

The findings from this research suggest that children who fare poorly in performance-related musical tasks can still achieve highly in listening-based activities. Should the music curriculum be differentiated to take this into account? Do we have the right balance between performance and listening in the music curriculum? Are there genuine equal opportunities in class or do we unconsciously bias our lessons in favour of musical children? These are challenging questions that need to be asked if optimum musical development is to be achieved and early disaffection from pupils who perceive themselves as unmusical avoided. Sadly, many research projects sit on library shelves gathering dust rather than being of real value to the practising primary teacher in the classroom. There is a growing need for 'real-world' research, relevant to issues affecting the everyday lives of practising teachers in the classroom. Hopefully more teachers will undertake similar projects, rooted in, and relevant to, the 'real world' of the classroom to bridge the 'invisible divide' between the academic research world and the classroom teacher. Such a partnership can only benefit all those concerned with the advancement of primary education.

## Useful further reading

*Enhancing Self Esteem in the Classroom*, D. Lawrence (1998). London: Chapman.

A readable and essential text for anyone wanting to know more about self-esteem. Lawrence takes self-image as the starting point of understanding and describes how low self-esteem can be disguised in many other forms of behaviour.

*Music in the Primary School*, J. Mills (1991). Cambridge: Cambridge University Press.

A good text for the music shelf of the staff room, thought provoking and dealing with real-world issues facing music teachers in the 1990s.

*Music, Society and Education*, C. Small (1984). London: Calder.

A useful book that focuses on cultural differences affecting music in society. It defends the all-round development of musical experience in non-Western societies and questions whether our 'classics' actually hinder progress in music making because their 'perfection' is idolised.

*Psychology in the Classroom*, P. Salmon (1995). London: Cassell.

Written especially for teachers, it presents the psychology of personal constructs in readable, meaningful language that is relevant to the 'real world' of the classroom. An inspiring book with profound implications for teaching and learning.

# References

Carlton, M. (1987) *Music in Education*. London: Woburn Press.

Dolgin, K. G. and Adelson, E. H. (1990) 'Age changes in the ability to interpret affect in sung and instrumentally presented melodies', *Psychology of Music* **18**(1), 87–98.

Gilbert, L. (1990) 'Aesthetic development in music: an experiment in the use of personal construct theory', *British Journal of Music* **7**(3), 173–90.

Giomo, C. J. (1993) 'An experimental study of children's sensitivity to mood in music', *Psychology of Music* **21**(2), 143–59.

Hentschke, L. (1993) 'Musical development: testing a model in the audience listening section' unpublished Ph.D. thesis, London Institute of Education.

Lawrence, D. (1988) *Enhancing Self Esteem in the Classroom*. London: Chapman.

Kastner, M. P. and Crowder, R. G. (1990) 'Perception of the major/minor distinction: emotional connotations in young children', *Music Perception* **8**(1), 189–202.

Kellet, M. C. (1998) *An exploratory study of ways to enhance young children's listening skills and raise self esteem*. Unpublished MA Thesis, Oxford Brookes University.

Kelly, G. (1955) *The Psychology of Personal Constructs*. New York: Norton.

Kratus, J. (1993) 'A developmental study of children's interpretations of emotion in music', *Psychology of Music* **21**(1), 3–18.

Mills, J. (1991) *Music in the Primary School*. Cambridge: Cambridge University Press.

Nisbett, J. and Watt, J. (1987) *Case Study*. Nottingham: Nottingham University School of Education.

Salmon, P. (1995) *Psychology in the Classroom*. London: Cassell.

Swanwick, K. and Tillman, J. (1986) 'The sequence of musical development: a study of children's composition', *British Journal of Music Education* **3**(3), 305–39.

Terwogt, M. M. and Van Grinsven, F. (1991) 'Musical expressions of mood states', *Psychology of Music* **19**(2), 99–109.

Vygotsky, L. (1962) *Thought and Language* (transl. Haufmann & Vakar). Cambridge, Mass.: MIT Press.

Ward, D. (1984) 'Personal construct theory: its application to research in music education and therapy', in Ross, M. (ed.) *Assessment in Arts Education: A Necessary Discipline or a Loss of Happiness?*, 197–209. Oxford and New York: Pergamon Press.

**Music link resource: Photocopiable pattern choice sheet**

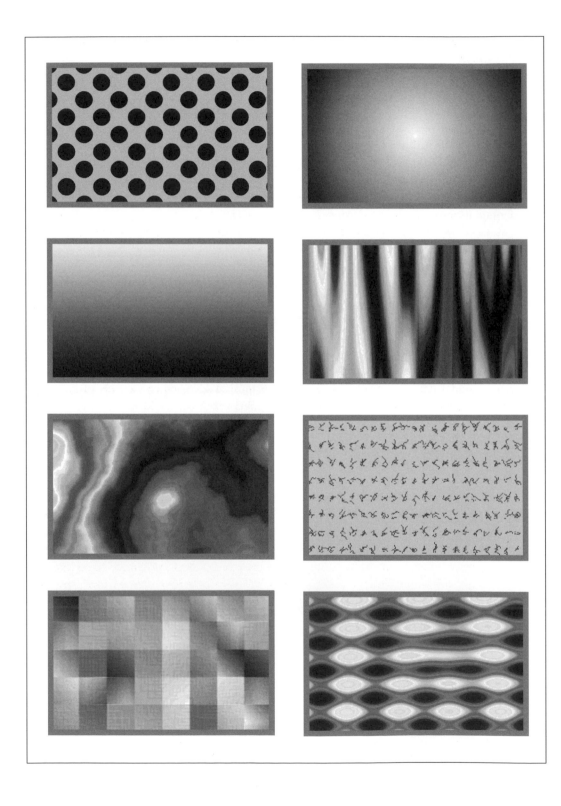

*Chapter 14*

# Demystifying the core strands in the National Curriculum for physical education

*Chris Carpenter*

In this chapter I have attempted to deconstruct the Core Strands (formerly called the Attainment Target) in the new National Curriculum for physical education by reporting on two pieces of research. Although both projects are based in secondary schools, the issues are relevant to primary schools and it is anticipated that these will make useful reading for primary teachers. I have included a practical activity based on the exemplar units of work that accompany the revised National Curriculum (2000) as non-statutory support. The practical activity emphasises the opportunities for children to be engaged in the activities of the core strands and focuses on teaching methodology to allow the core strands to be taught. I have also linked it with qualities that constitute the behaviours that a good learner in physical education should exhibit.

## Introduction

The idea of an attainment target for physical education was first proposed in the government's interim report (DES 1991: 25). The interim report proposed three attainment targets for physical education. These were planning, performing and evaluating. Although the attainment target has been subject to a good deal of refinement in the subsequent reforms the elements of planning, performing and evaluating have been kept. In the new National Curriculum the attainment target is referred to as the 'Core Strands', these being:

- acquiring and developing skills;
- selecting and applying skills, strategies, tactics and compositional ideas;
- evaluating and improving; and
- knowledge and understanding of fitness and health.

A criticism of the original attainment target was that planning, performing and evaluating were proposed as separate. Learning is a process of constant reconstruction so while planning, performing and evaluating have relevance they are not discrete but, in good learners, fully integrated.

The performing section of the attainment target has, unsurprisingly met with approval and understanding by most teachers, but there has been much discussion regarding what exactly is meant by planning and evaluating and it seems that there has been considerable variation in the ways that teachers have interpreted the ways that these two elements occur; in some cases they have been largely ignored. It is my contention that planning and evaluating are essential ingredients of learning in physical education and possibly other subjects as well. I am also suggesting that children must have the chance to put these processes into action in order to get better at them.

I would also suggest that it is important for teachers to begin to foster a culture of being a good learner in physical education. What kind of things does a good learner do? In the same way that there is a culture in physical education of encouraging all children to be good at exercising regularly, we should work towards a culture of everyone being a good learner. In other words, while good performance is the main goal, planning and evaluating are equally essential ingredients of this process. These should be three discrete concepts, and arguably it was a mistake in the early days of the National Curriculum for physical education to present them as one.

The problem for teachers is to develop teaching strategies that allow children to be able to plan, perform and evaluate naturally as part of the lesson, to enhance performance, and not as an artificial bolt-on just to satisfy a government dictate. The problem is not so much allowing planning and evaluating to occur but to assess and record children's' progress in these elements accurately, if indeed we need to.

In this chapter I will present two pieces of research that have investigated teachers' perceptions of the elements of the attainment target. Both pieces of research were undertaken in secondary schools. The findings indicate that there is a good deal of confusion among specialist secondary teachers, who are often able to focus on one subject. To primary teachers physical education is one of around ten subjects and so it seems likely that there will be confusion here also.

Finally I will present a unit of work in striking and fielding based on the non-statutory units of work that accompany the new National Curriculum. The unit will include the activities in progression and suggestions regarding organisation and teacher behaviour, which I suggest will allow children to have ample opportunities to plan, perform and evaluate.

## Research evidence

There have been a number of projects to investigate teacher's perceptions of planning, performing and evaluating. Two of the better-known pieces of research are explored here. The first (Crutchley and Robinson 1996) arose out of a concern by lecturers at Sheffield University, who found that students on teaching practice were encountering considerable variations in attitudes towards elements of the attainment target in the schools where they were carrying out their teaching practices, and that there was a great variety in emphasis between schools. This small-scale qualitative study involved data from nine secondary physical education teachers collected through a questionnaire. The teachers were all heads of department in 11–16 comprehensive schools.

The research method was to establish teachers' views by using questionnaires on the issues:

- definitions of the terms planning, performance and evaluating;
- activities undertaken as planning, performance and evaluating within games, gymnastics, dance, athletics and outdoor and adventurous activities; and
- the relative importance of planning, performance and evaluating within the curriculum as a whole.

The major findings were that while there were minor differences in the relative importance of planning, performance and evaluating, all respondents perceived 'performance' to be the key element of the assessment process. Perhaps this is a problem of the National Curriculum which Carroll (1994: 131) describes as an 'assessment driven curriculum'. All the teachers seemed to be working with intuitive and sometimes ill conceived notions of planning, performance and evaluating. None had written definitions and only one perceived a need for that level of precision. The findings concluded that there should be a greater dialogue about the nature of planning and evaluating and their reference to each area of the physical education curriculum.

The second study by Theodoulides and Armour (1998) was conducted in the London area. Six heads of physical education departments from different secondary schools were selected for a series of in-depth interpretative interviews. The respondents, three men and three women, were selected to include a range of teaching experience.

This study concluded that while the concept of 'performing' was relatively unproblematic, both 'planning' and 'evaluating' were fraught with practical and ideological difficulties. The authors suggest that the plan–perform–evaluate (PPE) cycle is too simplistic. Performance represents the educational worth of the National Curriculum for physical education. It is important for teachers to have a rationale to explain planning, performance and evaluating, and not attempt to create opportunities in an artificial way.

## The current situation

At the time of writing the new National Curriculum orders for implementation in September 2000 are being drafted for consultation. Table 14.1 shows a comparison between the attainment target in the current orders and the core strands in the new orders.

**Table 14.1** A comparison of the core strands in the new National Curriculum orders with the core strands in the current orders

| Core strands in new orders | Corresponding elements in current orders |
| --- | --- |
| Acquiring and developing skills | Performing |
| Selecting and applying skills, tactics and compositional ideas | Planning, performing |
| Evaluating and improving | Performing, evaluating |
| Knowledge and understanding of fitness and health | |

## Implications for teaching

The key issue for teachers is to structure activities so that the children have the opportunity to teach planning, performance and evaluating and allow that to happen in a natural way, which enhances the performance of the activity. There is a kind of golden triangle, which must be addressed at the planning stage in order to ensure that children's learning is effective (see Figure 14.1). The activity must be appropriate and if possible flexible enough to allow differentiation to occur easily. The teacher must have a clear idea of what constitutes good learning behaviour from the children and have a range of appropriate teaching methods to use to allow the learning to take place.

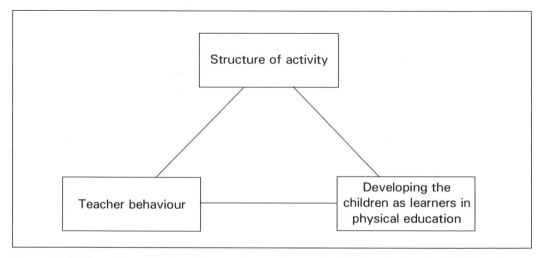

**Figure 14.1** The golden triangle of factors that underpin effective learning in physical education

### *Helping children to be good learners in physical education*

The key point here is that children must have the chance to make decisions for themselves. It is only through not being able to do something that we become able to do it. It is also crucial that children have the opportunity to evaluate and for their evaluations to inform future practice. In this way the core strands may be seen as totally integrated into the way that children learn in physical education and the process of evaluating becomes meaningful to them as learners and over a period of time will aid them in becoming better learners in physical education.

It is important that teachers have a view on what learning behaviour is required by children in order to become good learners in physical education. Fisher (1995: 125) refers to a mastery orientation as a sense of self-efficacy or self-competence and suggests eight characteristics, which if nurtured successfully with children will empower them to be successful learners in physical education:

- willingness to try hard tasks;
- ability to view problems as a challenge;
- ability to accept failure without excuse;

- flexibility in approach;
- being self-motivated by learning;
- wanting to achieve learning goals;
- having a positive view of learning; and
- ability to cooperate and compete.

Children will come to physical education lessons with a range of differing expectations and experiences in physical activity, but it is crucial to try to nurture children to have a mastery orientation by emphasising small points such as how normal mistakes are and that they are a normal part of learning. Children who mock other children when they make mistakes must be corrected by the teacher immediately. It is vital to ensure an atmosphere in the class where the children feel safe to risk, try and fail, but will keep trying. When I am faced with a new class I often play games with them to learn their names and when I make mistakes emphasise to them that now I am a learner and that they must be supportive of me in my attempts to learn their names; so modelling the behaviour of a good learner.

The old argument of whether physical education is an education of the physical or through the physical is worth considering here. A recent study by Laker (1996) found that student teachers felt they were more complete teachers if they could deliver all of the aims that they were required to deliver. The generic groupings identified were sportsmanship, cooperation, individual and attitudes.

## Link resource

To demonstrate these ideas in practice I am recommending a game that has been designed to demonstrate *how* planning and evaluating might be integrated into a generic striking and fielding game. The same pitch set-up may be used for a simple game suitable for use with Key Stage 1 children, or can be adapted for use with Key Stage 2 children.

I have presented the game as a series of progressions, which will straddle Key Stages 1 and 2. The idea that the curriculum is a spiral one where pupils constantly revisit skills and tactical themes is very much in line with the most recent ideas of how children learn. Bennett and Dunne (1984: 50) point out that what children learn in school will depend to a large extent on what they already know.

### Teacher behaviour

Mosston and Ashworth's (1994: 103–15) self-check style may be used to support this style, with the teacher asking the children questions to highlight the aims: 'What were you trying to do?', 'Would you say that it worked?' This is a useful way to direct the children's attention to the most crucial points without giving them the answer. It also a simple way to encourage them to evaluate themselves and to stress that their evaluation should inform their next attempt. The teachers comments might go along the lines of: 'Why did you try to hit the ball over the fielders?', 'You have been caught twice now', 'What else could you do?'

## Prior learning

One of the strengths of the non-statutory units of work that accompany the new National Curriculum is the idea of prior learning, which is essential to underpin the game. In this case I suggest that the following activities should have been pursued and that the children have a good understanding of their skills and concepts:

- catching activities;
- rolling activities;
- throwing activities; and
- the concept of racing.

In addition, for the variations where the pupils are striking the ball with a bat there are three stages that need to have been taught and practised:

- hitting the ball off a tee;
- hitting the ball off a bounce, or even two – the ball is still at the top of a bounce and so easier to hit; and
- hitting the ball on the full or on the volley.

## The game

To demonstrate how teachers might integrate planning and evaluation into children's physical education activities, I will outline a generic striking and fielding game. Clearly this can be adapted for Key Stage 1 and 2 children, but perhaps more importantly it should be recognised that the purpose of the lesson plan is to illustrate the integration of skills. In other words it is intended as a process model, rather than a definitive lesson. The different stages of the game are shown in Figure 14.2. The pitch is a home base with two bases, which branch out from it (Figure 14.3). When I have presented it to children they often think that they are not allowed to hit the ball beyond the bases. In order to try to describe this better when I asked a class teacher in a primary school that I was working with she came up with the idea of referring to it as a slice of cake. When setting the game up I always pick a target in the distance such as a road, building or trees and say that as long as the ball has travelled between the bases in the area then as far as possible is fine.

## Adaptations and developments

As in all subject areas, it is important for teachers to have strategies for differentiation in physical education. This may occur by outcome with the better players being more successful but I would suggest that there are a number of 'differentiation by design' strategies that are worth considering.

When the children reach the point where they are striking the ball make sure that the activity is geared to the children being successful. It always seems to me that rounders was designed by someone who was determined to give children as little chance of success at games as possible. Can you imagine a smaller ball or a more difficult bat? There are many alternatives. Short tennis rackets, stoolball bats and mini cricket bats are all good alternatives that will allow the ball to be struck easily. It is also crucial to set the striking activity

## Stage 1

**Activity (pitch set up as in Figure 14.3):** Batter rolls the ball into the slice of cake. The batter then races the remainder of the group who have to get the ball back to the home base before the batter can get around the bases. The batter must return to the home base before the fielders can put the ball into the marker on the home base marker.

**Development:** As above but the batter throws the ball. Pitch width may be varied according to ability of the children in a particular group or if a game with fewer children is required (see Figure 14.4c).

**Selecting and applying skills, strategies, tactics and compositional ideas (planning)**

**Batters:** Batter thinks about how they will roll or throw the ball. They must remember key points of rolling and throwing from practice.

**Teacher:** Encourage batters to aim for gaps and/or vary the speed of the roll or throw. Reminds batters of key points when throwing/rolling. Makes suggestions as to where the ball might be thrown or rolled.

**Fielders:** Children decide where they will stand.

**Teacher:** Asking children questions such as should they stand in the same place for all batters? Is it best to run with the ball or relay it to the home base?

**Evaluating and improving**

**Batters:** The teacher should help the children to evaluate by asking them questions such as how did they get on using a particular roll or throw? How successful were they in the place that they aimed? Did it go as planned? How will it affect your next attempt?

**Fielders:** The teacher should help the children by asking questions such as did the places that you stood in work? How could it be better? What will you do next time?

## Stage 2

**Activity (use pitch set-up in Figure 14.3):** Batter hits the ball into the slice of cake. Batter may use any of the three methods to feed the ball for themselves to hit.

**Development:** Use pitch set-up Figure 14.4b. Batter must attempt a rounder or home run every hit. They score one point if they get to Base 1, two points if they get to Base 2 and three points for Base 3. If they get all the way around then they score five points. They are allowed to stop at any base and there is no penalty for being 'run out'. Once they have passed the base they get the point(s) for passing that base. The fielders may run the batter out at any base. This encourages the fielders to have to make decisions regarding which base they will throw to.

**Selecting and applying skills, strategies, tactics and compositional ideas (planning)**

**Batters:** Batter thinks about how they will hit the ball. They must remember key points from practice. Encourage them to aim for gaps and/or vary the speed hit. If you want to make sure that you are not caught out then hit the ball along the floor.

**Figure 14.2** Different stages of generic striking and fielding game (continued overleaf)

**Teacher:** Reminds batters of key points when throwing/rolling. Makes suggestions as to where the ball might be hit.

**Fielders:** Encourage children to think about the outcomes. Should they stand in the same place for all batters? Is it best to run with the ball or relay it to the home base? Does it make any difference if the batter is left- or right-handed?

**Teacher:** Teacher questions children about their field placings.

### Evaluating and improving

**Batters:** Teacher reminds children that they have a choice of types of hitting. How did they get on using a particular roll or throw? How successful were they in the place that they aimed? Did it go as planned? How will it affect their next attempt?

**Fielders:** Teacher reminds children about choices they have regarding field placings. Did the places they stood work? How could it be better? How will what happened affect their next attempt?

## Stage 3

**Activity:** Pupils work in pairs. One of the pair feeds the ball for their partner to hit. Encourage the children to work together in order to find the best way for the ball to be fed. Scoring may be as in Stage 2 but the scores of the pair are added together. Batter hits the ball into the slice of cake.

### Selecting and applying skills, strategies, tactics and compositional ideas (planning)

**Batters and feeder:** Batter thinks about how they want the ball fed to them to hit the ball. Batter should think about where the ball is hit.

**Teacher:** Encourage feeder and batter to experiment to find the best way to hit and feed. Reminds pairs that they are working together. What does it mean to be a good partner in physical education? Make suggestions as to how the ball might be fed. Encourage the batter to ask for the ball to be fed as they would prefer.

**Fielders:** Think about where they stand. Make plans of what to do in different situations. Try to organise the ball to be relayed to bases.

**Teacher:** Encourage children to think about the outcomes. Should they stand in the same place for all batters? Is it best to run with the ball or relay it to the home base? Does it make any difference if the batter is right- or left-handed?

### Evaluating and improving

**Batters:** Teacher questions the pupils asking how they got on using a particular way of feeding the ball? How successful were they in the place that they aimed? How does where the ball is fed affect the ease of hitting to a particular spot? Did it go as planned? How will it affect their next attempt?

**Fielders:** Teacher questions children about the field placing. Did the places they stood work? How could it be better?

**Figure 14.2**    Different stages of generic striking and fielding game

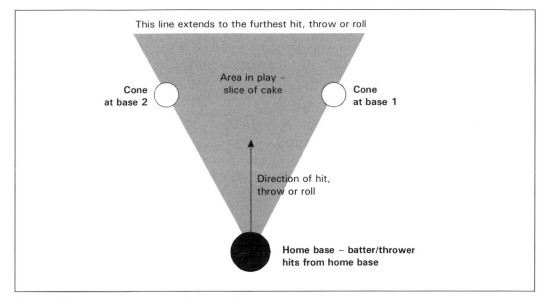

**Figure 14.3** Basic pitch set-up (the slice of cake)

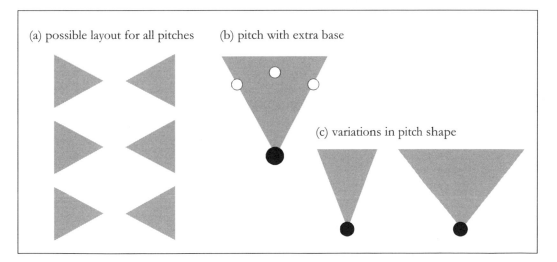

**Figure 14.4** Pitch variations

up in such a way that they ball can be struck. Hitting a larger ball along the ground is perfectly acceptable. Hitting off a tee, feeding the ball for themselves are good methods, which will allow children to build confidence in striking a ball.

Grouping of children is also a good way to ensure that they are working as close to their limits as possible. Setting the groups so that the more capable play in different games to the less able is a good way to achieve this. If the space is limited then use a ball which will not fly too far. I have worked with primary schools where the only outdoor space is a small yard. Sponge balls can be used which can be struck as hard as possible but will not fly far and do not pose a threat to windows!

The size of the 'piece of cake' may be varied according to the capability of the class and the space available (Figure 14.4). Better players may be given a wider space if the emphasis is on stretching the fielders or a narrower space if the pressure is to be placed upon the batter. Small changes to a game can have major considerations for the children and enhance the need for planning and evaluating to inform their performance. A classic example of this is changing the ball to one that flies slowly. The thinking player realising that if they attempt to go over the top will be caught has to manufacture ways to hit the ball along the ground in order to ensure that they get the ball into play safely.

## Conclusions

In this chapter I have identified an area that has been subject to a good deal of discussion in the implementation of the National Curriculum for physical education. The guidelines to the new orders refer to the 'thinker's curriculum'. I believe that it is important to develop children as good learners in physical education and this requires not only teaching them skills and concepts but teaching them what it is to be a good learner and then giving them the chance to practise this so that they can approach any physical activity with confidence.

I believe that this requires the use of appropriate activities with the children being encouraged not only to learn the activity and develop confidence but that the process of thinking about what is happening and evaluating it in a simple but immediate way to inform future practice should be fostered by the teacher. This will not necessarily just happen and teachers must develop their own behaviour in order to highlight the opportunities for thoughtful work in lessons. Intelligence has great cachet in our society and in school in particular. There is a feeling that physical competence is innate and not clever. I would argue that this is not the case. Howard Gardner's work on multiple intelligences is well known and worth reading. Garner identifies bodily-kinaesthetic intelligence, which he describes as follows: 'This intelligence describes the abilities to use the body or parts of the body to solve problems or to produce worthwhile products or displays. It involves at its core the capacities to control bodily motions and to handle objects skilfully' Gardner (1994: 40).

When good work is carried out in lessons I always call the children 'clever'. Clever is an adjective that we all like to have applied to us. In a time when boys' under-achievement in schools is a cause for concern, perhaps acknowledging all children's achievements in physical education as clever and worthwhile might have positive effects and benefit them in all areas of the curriculum.

## Useful further reading

*Striking and Fielding Games*, J. Severs (1994). Hemel Hempstead: Simon and Schuster.

A well laid out book, which examines the principles of play with examples of the different families of striking and fielding games.

*Teaching Children to Learn*, R. Fisher (1995). Cheltenham: Stanley Thornes (Publishers).

Fisher outlines ten ways to help children learn. While the book is primarily aimed at children's learning in the classroom, many of the principles apply equally in a practical subject such as physical education.

*The Effective Teaching of Physical Education*, M. Mawer (1995). London: Longman.

This is a book written by a well known teacher trainer of physical education, which covers all the areas of physical education teaching from philosophy through teaching strategies to assessment.

*Physical Education in the Early Years*, P. Wetton (1997). London: Routledge.

A comprehensive introduction into the whole area of physical education for Key Stages 1 and 2 by one of the most respected authors in the area. Each chapter covers the activity areas, comes with examples of activities and is linked to the NCPE guidelines.

# References

Bennet, N. and Dunne, E. (1994) 'How children learn: implications for practice', in B. Moon and A. Shelton Mayes (eds) *Teaching and Learning in the Secondary School*, 50–6. London: Routledge.

Carroll, B. (1994) *Assessment in Physical Education: A Teacher's Guide to the Issues*. London: Falmer Press.

Crutchley, D. and Robinson, L. (1996) 'Teachers' perceptions of "planning", "performing" and "evaluating" within the National Curriculum Physical Education', *Bulletin of Physical Education* **32**(1), 46–54.

Department of Education and Science (DES) (1991) *Interim Report of the National Curriculum: Physical Education Working Group*. London: HMSO.

Fisher, R. (1995) *Teaching Children to Learn*. Cheltenham: Stanley Thornes.

Gardner, H. (1984) 'The theory of multiple intelligences', in Moon,. B. and A. Shelton Mayes (eds) *Teaching and Learning in the Secondary School*. London: Routledge.

Laker, A. (1996) 'Learning to teach through the physical as well as of the physical', *The British Journal of Physical Education* **27**(4), 18–22.

Mosston, M. and Ashworth, S. (1992) *Teaching Physical Education*. New York: MacMillan Publishing Company.

Theodoulides, A. and Armour,K. (1998) 'Planning, performing and evaluating in National Curriculum Physical Education: a critical review', *European Journal of Physical Education* **3**(2), 129–44.

**Physical education link resource: Teacher checklist**

Do I provide the children with the chance to practise the prior learning that underpins striking and fielding games?
*Skills such as catching, throwing, hitting and stopping.*

Do my children have the chance to work with a ball each regularly? *Just watch the confidence in catching grow!*

How might I use adapted implements?
*Short tennis rackets are ideal. Spend time with the children hitting only.*

Am I ensuring that the groups are small enough to ensure maximum participation?
*Maximum of five is suggested.*

How might I encourage the children to think about their next attempt (ie planning)?

- *Is that the best place to stand when Claire is batting?*
- *Where are you aiming the ball on this hit?*
- *Why did you aim it there?*
- *Why did you run to that base to run the batter out? You could have thrown it to Sam.*

How might I encourage the children to evaluate their work and use the evaluations to inform future work?

- *Was that a good place to stand when Claire was batting?*
- *Did you aim the ball there? Why did you do that? What could you do next time?*
- *When the ball came to you why did you throw it to Sam? Would you say that worked? What could you do next time?*

*Chapter 15*

# Researching skills common to religious education and citizenship

*Nick Mead*

This chapter seeks to identify pedagogic skills that are common to religious education and citizenship. The research findings highlight the processes which teachers should be encouraged to engage with if such skills are to be developed in the classroom. The conclusion reached is that attention paid to the development of such skills may begin to address the notion of an, as yet, unfulfilled broad and balanced curriculum which contributes to children's moral and spiritual growth.

## Background

Hobson and Edwards (1999) have shown how religious education is being challenged to go beyond an understanding of religions to providing skills of critical reflection and evaluation which will enable children to interpret and make sense of our pluralistic world. This challenge to religious education has coincided with the emergence of a global concern for the moral nature of citizenship. The School Curriculum and Assessment Authority's (SCAA) MORI poll (1996: 20–2) which informed the Crick Report (Advisory Group on Citizenship (AGC) (1998) showed that young people are interested in moral questions but are cynical about political leadership.

The challenge to religious education to become more reflective and evaluative in its approach to beliefs and values and the coincident concern for the moral nature of citizenship brings into sharp relief the nature of the relationship between religious education and citizenship within the primary curriculum. This is not only a philosophical issue but also a practical one, bearing in mind that the Crick Report recommends five per cent of curriculum time for citizenship in an already crowded curriculum.

Concern about teacher and pupil skills within citizenship pedagogy came to the fore in the Crick Report consultation process, following the first draft of the report. Those consulted expressed a need for teachers to have 'The confidence, knowledge and skills to be able to deliver effective Citizenship education' (AGC 1998: 75). In relation to pupils' skills, the point was made that in some cases the culture of a school might need to change to enable pupils to be given opportunities to reflect and critically evaluate. Participants in the consultation exercise wanted further clarification about the relationship between citizenship education and other subject areas and the spiritual, moral, social and cultural. In the light of the development of skills in reflection, application and evaluation in religious education, it would seem logical to look to existing good practice in that subject within a school for exemplification of pupil and teacher skills in citizenship.

The Crick Report has three strands, the first of which may be described as moral development: 'Children learning from the very beginning self-confidence and socially and morally responsible behaviour both in and beyond the classroom, both towards those in authority and towards each other' (AGC 1998: 11, para. 2.11). The report makes the important point that the whole of primary education is not pre-citizenship; children are already forming, through learning and discussion, concepts of fairness, and attitudes to the law, to rules, to decision-making, to authority, to their local environment and social responsibility.

The research of Hughes (1975 cited in Bottery (1990: 63–5)) has demonstrated that children could make sense of what they were asked to do in his 'hiding from the policeman' moral task because they know what it is to hide from somebody – it is part of their experience and they can become involved in it. Piagetian moral tests by contrast can be artificial, abstract and outside the children's experience. Such research benefits the development of skills in religious education and citizenship because it suggests that moral development is a product of social communication and that one of the crucial roles of the teacher is to provide guidance for the child in the structuring and facilitating of communication situations.

Here we can begin to see the mutual benefits to be gained from pursuing a relationship between religious education and citizenship. The concept of the primary classroom as the 'community of inquiry' developed by Matthew Lipman (1991) provides a good model for both curriculum areas. There is a need in religious education to use moral and religious narrative out of which pupils identify key issues they wish to discuss in order to achieve learning *from* religions (QCA 1994: Target 2). The skills of empathy, reflective, application and evaluation associated with Attainment Target 2 in religious education correspond to skills identified in the Crick Report from Key Stage 1 onwards:

- The ability to make a reasoned argument both verbally and in writing
- Ability to consider and appreciate the experience and perspective of others
- Ability to tolerate other viewpoints
- Ability to develop a problem-solving approach
- A critical approach to evidence put before one and ability to look for fresh evidence
- Ability to identify, respond to and influence moral challenges and situations

(QCA 1998: 44)

The social communication facilitated by the model of the 'community of inquiry' not only develops skills common to religious education and citizenship but also key attitudes crucial to positive moral development. The QCA model syllabuses and probably most recently revised local agreed syllabuses refer to the attitudes of commitment to a set of values by which to live one's life; fairness in terms of giving careful consideration to other views; respect for those who hold different beliefs and avoiding ridicule; self-understanding, including a sense of self-worth and value and finally, a positive attitude of enquiry which includes a readiness to change one's point of view. There is much here that is common with the values and dispositions identified in the Crick Report:

- Belief in human dignity and equality.
- Judging and acting by a moral code.
- Courage to defend a point of view.
- The practice of tolerance.
- Willingness to be open to challenging one's opinion and attitudes in the light of discussion and evidence                    (AGC 1998: 44)

To conclude our examination of the first strand of the Crick Report we can say that exemplification of good practice in moral development may be already in place within a school's religious education programme. If an audit of skills in moral development show this not to be the case, then let the implementation of citizenship be the catalyst to improve the quality of religious education!

The second strand of the Crick Report is community involvement : 'Children learning about and becoming helpfully involved in the life and concerns of their communities, including learning through community involvement and service to the community' (AGC 1998: para. 2.11b).

One of the key points emerging from the Crick Report consultation process was that teachers need to take into account the local context in which schools would be teaching about citizenship and democracy. The local context is also crucial in the formation of the religious education scheme of work and and it is a legal requirement that the policy document clearly relates the aims of the subject to the local needs. What can be learnt from the distinctively local organisation of religious education which will complement this second strand of citizenship?

The close relationship between religious education and the local community encourages teachers to use visits and visitors which, if done well, help to develop many of the moral and social skills common to religious education and citizenship.The emphasis on learning *from* religions corresponds very much to the Crick use of learning *through* community involvement. The most effective use of religious education visits and visitors involves dialogue between the children and members of the faith communities which encourages empathy, reflection and evaluation and in turn develops positive attitudes of respect, fairness and enquiry. Again, are the pedagogic skills to facilitate open dialogue with community members in place already in religious education? If not then let citizenship be the inspiration to make this happen.

The third strand of the Crick Report is political literacy: 'Children learning how to make themselves effective in public life through knowledge, skills and values. Political literacy is wider than political knowledge alone. It encompasses preparation for conflict resolution and decision-making in relation to the economic and social problems of the day' (AGC 1998: 13, para. 211). Political literacy in democratic education promotes spiritual, moral and intellectual autonomy; this means that spiritual education is about engaging in dialogue with others who hold different values as part of the process of achieving spiritual autonomy. It involves self-understanding in terms of the value of the individual in relation to the community. For religious education, spiritual autonomy and the value of the individual is at the heart of political literacy. It follows that pedagogic skills in facilitating children's spiritual development is at the heart of religious education and citizenship.

Hay and Nye (1998) have been able to identify for teachers the conditions, processes and strategies which facilitate spiritual development; conditions such as religious language, the language of beliefs and the language of fiction, the processes of interiorising, self-identification and the strategies of philosophising, reasoning and moralising. Clearly, creating such conditions involves the skills of learning *from* religions in particular and the skills of citizenship such as the ability to respond to and influence social, moral and political challenges which impinge on the spiritual dignity and autonomy of the individual citizen.

The international trend towards inter-cultural discourse in religious education and concern about the moral dimensions of citizenship have led to an examination of the three strands of the Crick Report in terms of skills common to both curriculum areas. Having identified common skills we now turn to research evidence which suggests ways in which schools might develop them.

## Action research

The action research which follows is based on course evaluations from two cohorts passing through a new citizenship final year BEd elective. The ongoing processes by which we evaluate ITT courses is a type of action research which should be made more use of, particularly when such courses are responding to TTA requirements which in turn reflect curriculum innovation affecting the professional development of all primary teachers. In the absence of any substantial research on citizenship in ITT it seemed essential to reflect with the trainees on the training process and extrapolate principles of good training which might inform future INSET for serving teachers. This reflective process was also to take into account that some of the trainees would become religious education or citizenship coordinators and would be able to use these principles of good practice in their planning and staff development.

The research focuses on the processes involved in primary trainee teachers becoming aware of and developing confidence in a set of pedagogic skills common to religious education and citizenship. Data collection involved the following.

- A course evaluation sheet was given to the 20 members of the first cohort. The sections invited reflections on the following:
  1. To what extent have the course aims been met?
  2. What evidence have you of the desirable learning outcomes?
  3. What do you consider to be the strengths of the course?
  4. What do you consider to be the weaknesses of the course?
  5. What suggestions would you make for developing the course?
- A reflective piece of writing was requested in response to the following: 'Trainee teachers need to think and talk about their values before entering the classroom if they are not to pass on their own values uncritically'.
- The second cohort of 17 trainees were asked to reflect on the kind of INSET they would like a citizenship coordinator to provide to develop teacher self-concept.

The responses were analysed and categories of response identified and from these key findings were extrapolated. The evaluation analysis was categorised according to the questions; the reflective piece of writing was categorised according to pedagogic skills and the INSET suggestions fell into categories of approach. Small-scale action research of this kind primarily benefits reflective practice and practical planning within a specific context. It does provide a model of good practice in the context of religious education and citizenship as both areas require pedagogic skills of reflection, application and evaluation.

## The findings

### Finding 1

The areas of beliefs and values and spiritual and moral development often go unspoken and are areas in which teachers often lack confidence. The data indicates trainees experiencing uncertainty about how schools handle values and a desire to be told which values to espouse:

> There is currently too little research literature written by too narrow a range of authors to provide a theoretical assurance to our beliefs. We are still lacking an accepted criteria of what society's values are and until both of these missing aspects are improved and available the Citizenship course will only help us understand individual's values and be of no broader benefit than that.
>
> (Trainee O)

This raises the challenging question about whether schools are in the business of transmitting values, clarifiying values or providing a framework of core values within which children can securely reflect on and evaluate the range of values encountered in a pluralistic society and modify their own values in the process. The course evaluations indicate that although initially seeking the kind of assurance expressed by Trainee O, trainees progress from recognising the limitations of approaches one and two to growing confidence in handling approach three. This is expressed in their assessment of their own experience of the third approach on the course:

> This course gives depth to teachers which may otherwise be missing in their training. So much time is spent on acquiring and imparting knowledge. A greater understanding of Citizenship and related values enables teachers to be more well-rounded and hopefully better teachers.        (Trainee E)

Another trainee takes this further and makes the connection between the confidence gained through her own experience of the third approach on the course and the significant recognition that the classroom is not a value-free zone:

> It would have been extremely helpful to have been given time to have had Citizenship lectures much earlier in the course as it is something which should be an integral part of your time in school. I have certainly benefited (and I hope my pupils have) from re-assessing and re-evaluating my own values and the values I aspire to demonstrate in the classroom.        (Trainee L)

A fourth trainee links the processes of reassessing and re-evaluating with a pluralistic values-laden classroom:

> The elective has helped me to understand and realise the importance of being aware of different values amongst staff, pupils and parents and how one might deal with them. We are not always aware of how these different values are influencing the children who encounter us.     (Trainee A)

It is evident that this first finding is at the heart of the trainees' intellectual understanding of how school should approach beliefs and values and the spiritual and moral. This intellectual understanding has been gained through their own experience on the course of an approach which is secure, formative and inclusive and has none of the polarisation of values clarification and values transmission.

*Finding 2*

Trainees recognised the value of, but have had limited opportunities to develop skills in philosophical inquiry and moral reasoning. The data highlight two key responses. Firstly, there is real appreciation of the opportunity to activate these dormant skills, albeit at the eleventh hour of the course! Trainee evaluations of the course aims emphasised positive 'opportunities for thoughtful reflection on values in the classroom'; their evaluations of learning outcomes from the course highlighted how, 'during the course we have developed skills in reflective discussion, moral reasoning and philosophical inquiry'; the strengths of the course were identified as 'opportunities for discussion and time to reflect', 'an expression of much that is unspoken', and 'ways into the teaching of values which develops these as part of the professional and personal development of the teacher'. Trainees' written reflections on the course highlighted how they had deepened their reflective skills and how this had increased their awareness of the need for skills in open dialogue:

> The elective has given me the opportunity to think about and reflect on my own beliefs. I think I now have a greater awareness of my influence (or potential influence) on the children in my care. Teachers who are not made explicitly aware of the need to have an 'open mind' when it comes to to teaching children may find that they are not giving due care or attention to children's spiritual, moral, social and cultural care and education.     (Trainee D)

Secondly, trainees expressed some dismay at how such skills have not been integral to a four-year training process. Trainee course evaluations recommended that the personal and social education elective be retained and introduced over years three and four of the four-year course. In trainees' written reflections on the course there is evidence of a recognition that the skills of philosophical inquiry and moral reasoning ought to underpin the intensive and often dominating ITT National Curriculum requirements: 'A broad curriculum is not merely teaching the ten National Curriculum subjects but an integral part of the utmost importance is to nurture the child's own set of values so that they can become better citizens' (Trainee F). These two aspects of Finding 2 do draw our attention to trends in ITT which we have been aware of as we have witnessed the emergence of a national curriculum for teacher training which mirrors something of the content-driven school curriculum. Are the challenges of making sense of our lives in pluralistic societies going to lead to a reconsideration of pedagogic skills?

*Finding3*
Trainees have become aware during the course that handling beliefs and values and the spiritual and moral requires the teacher to have self-understanding. Course evaluations picked up on the interrelatedness of teacher self-understanding, pupil self-understanding and professional practice within the structure of sessions. Trainees' reflective written comments suggest that developing self-understanding is part of an educational process and there is recognition of the need for differentiation: 'I believe it would be beneficial for other trainee teachers to be *educated* in this area of the curriculum' (Trainee H). 'An awareness needs to be highlighted. This may not be necessary for all but if it makes one person question their values then it is worth it. It is very important and needs to be made explicit' (Trainee K).

Teacher self-understanding is linked to confidence in the pedagogic skills we have identified as common to citizenship and learning *from* religions:

> Children will ask questions about values. It is essential that trainee teachers feel ready to be able to deal with these situations in a classroom and throughout the school. No one can be an effective model of values if the term is not understood thoroughly or the teachers do not have a clear picture of their own values. *If one is unsure of values that stand in the classroom and school then the children will be unsure.* (Trainee T)

This confidence seems to be derived from the process of making teachers' implicit values explicit and allowing them to be shaped by dialogue with others as part of a process in achieving moral and spiritual autonomy: 'Surely every teacher training course should include values education in order that the implicit might become explicit and children can benefit from confident teachers with clarified understandings' (Trainee J).

Spiritual and moral autonomy begins to emerge as teachers are invited to reflect on and evaluate their morals and values and to consider whether they are appropriate for the classroom: 'The course allows for reflection but also gives alternative views and suggestions about the values you hold' (Trainee I). The outcome of this process is related by one trainee directly to classroom ethos: 'Sharing opinions and looking at what others have said about values helps to give us confidence and new ideas for creating the kind of classroom ethos that we would like' (Trainee N).

The data supporting Finding 3 suggest that the lack of confidence in the whole citizenship area noted by SCAA (1996: 17) does relate to teacher self-understanding. Are we saying that if teachers are to be effective in this area they need to be aware of how they are achieving spiritual and moral autonomy as part of becoming full citizens?

*Finding 4*
Trainees are particularly aware of the relationship between teacher self-understanding and pupil self-understanding in religious education and citizenship. What is significant in the trainees' written reflections is the natural link made between teacher confidence derived from self-understanding and pupil confidence and raised self-esteem: 'I believe

that all trainee teachers need to develop an awareness of their own values from an early stage in their training. They should be aware of how these values affect their pupils and their response from their first practice and observation in school' (Trainee C). This awareness of the effect of our values on each other is likely to reflect the experience of dialogue within this elective group and it seems to have sensitised them to the process of achieving spiritual and moral autonomy. Their reflective comments suggest a heightened awareness of the same process of achieving autonomy among their pupils: 'All trainees should have the opportunity to learn about how values education improves a child's self-esteem. They should know the importance of this and how it shapes the children for their later lives' (Trainee G).

Denis Lawrence (1998) has identified the integral link between teacher and pupil self-concept and self-esteem; finding four points to a challenging dimension of this relationship, which is the raising of self-esteem through the teacher and pupil *sharing* the experience of achieving spiritual and moral autonomy.

## Implications for teaching

The four findings are helpful in providing ways forward in the development of pedagogic skills common to the areas of religious education and citizenship. Underpinning skills and confidence in these areas is the need for an intellectual understanding of how schools approach beliefs and values and the spiritual and moral. I suggest that such understanding comes from the kind of personal and professional development experienced by my elective students. Little time is given to dialogue between staff focused on how the school handles values. Without a series of such experiences in which teachers gain confidence in the processes of dialogue, the desired pedagogic skills cannot flourish.

Many teachers feel the tension between pupils wrestling with conflicting values and the pressure caused by the need to get on with the next task. Schools may now have a mandate to reconsider the range of pedagogic skills they are using and begin to develop expertise in moral reasoning and philosophical inquiry. If the intellectual understanding has been established it is likely that staff will welcome the kinds of INSET opportunities provided by Jenny Mosley's Circle Time and June Auton's Human Values Foundation. Such INSET opportunities do challenge staff to harness new pedagogic skills and may lead to the reviewing of whole school policies on religious education and citizenship.

Primary religious education specialists may be particularly aware of the part played by their own growth towards spiritual and moral autonomy. The Crick Report puts this clearly in the realm of political literacy as it involves an understanding of the value of the individual in relation to political and economic systems. There may be the opportunity now to develop this dimension in school as a result of the Crick Report and clearly the correlation suggested by the data is that teachers with a sense of their own spiritual and moral growth can effectively assist the same growth in their pupils. Values forums can be highly productive if focused around the aims and values of the school; this is an exercise which governors may wish to participate in as well. The teacher who is aware of their own moral and spiritual growth may be more ready to engage in philosophical and moral reflection with pupils.

Finally, there is the exciting but challenging dynamic in religious education and citizenship pedagogy which is a teacher/pupil shared experience of achieving spiritual and moral autonomy. This may be facilitated by the Matthew Lipman 'community of inquiry' ethos using moral narrative resources such as *You, Me, Us* (Home Office/Citizenship Foundation 1994). However, it is important that the teacher does not remain just as facilitator but may be open to expressing how their own views have been shaped by reflective dialogue with the pupils.

## Link resource

The resource arises from the four key findings and from a survey of elective students about the kind of INSET they would value in this area. The need would seem to be very much in the area of developing staff skills in reflective dialogue as part of the kind of self-evaluation exercise which LEAs and OFSTED will be expecting schools to undertake. The exercise may take more than one session and questions need to be explored in pairs, groups and in plenary.

## Conclusions

The introduction of citizenship into the curriculum may be an opportunity to firm up pedagogic skills which have been required in the areas of religious and personal and social education but which have not received sufficient attention. The identification of a common skills base across religious education and citizenship should not be seen as a threat to the former but rather as an opportunity to enhance the quality of teaching in both areas without detracting from their distinctive contributions. What we might hope for is that the introduction of citizenship does begin to address the unfulfilled expectation of a broad and balanced curriculum which does promote the spiritual and moral, social and cultural.

## Useful further reading

*Education for Human Values*, J. Auton (ed.) (1995). Ilminster: The Human Values Foundation.

This provides curriculum materials for implementing a whole school values education programme.

*Quality Circle Time in The Primary Classroom*, J. Mosley (1996). Wisbech: LDA.

This book offers one of the leading approaches to conducting circle time, and links it to developing dialogue between pupils.

*Discerning the Spirit: Teaching Spirituality in the Religious Education Classroom*, A. Wright (1999). Abingdon: Culham College Institute.

This is a practical user-friendly version of a more academic book that applies the theory of spiritual education to classroom practice.

# References

Advisory Group on Citizenship (AGC) (1998) *Education for Citizenship and the Teaching of Democracy in School* (the Crick Report). London: QCA.

Bottery, M. (1990) *The Morality of the School*. London: Cassell.

Hay, D. and Nye, R.(1998) *The Spirit of the Child*. London: HarperCollins.

Hobson, P. and Edwards, J. (1999) *Religious Education in a Pluralist Society*. London: Woburn Press.

Home Office/Citizenship Foundation (1994) *You, Me, Us*. London: Home Office.

Hughes, M. (1975) Egocentrism in Pre-school Children. Unpublished Ph.D. dissertation, University of Edinburgh.

Lawrence, D. (1988) *Enhancing Self-esteem in the Classroom*. London: Paul Chapman.

Lipman, M. (1991) *Thinking in Education*. Cambridge: Cambridge University Press.

School Curriculum and Assessment Authority (SCAA) (1994) *Religious Education Model Syllabuses*. London: SCAA.

School Curriculum and Assessment Authority (SCAA) (1996) *Education for Adult Life: The Spiritual and Moral Development of Young People*. London: SCAA.

**Religious education link resource: Staff self-assessment exercise and skills audit for the teaching of religious education and citizenship**

---

1. To what extent do we as a staff share the values of the school as stated in the school prospectus and in our mission statement?

2. Can we identify skills common to religious education and citizenship which might strengthen the values of the school?

3. How often do we give children time to reflect on a belief or value and how often do we invite them to give reasoned points of view?

4. Can you think of an occasion when children developed their moral outlook as a result of having dialogues with one another?

5. What does being a citizen mean to me?

6. Do I feel that I am developing morally and spiritually as a citizen?

7. How often are my own moral and spiritual views developed or modified as a result of having dialogues with children?

# Glossary

**Action research**   A practical form of enquiry through which practitioners can observe and reflect on phenomena within their own situation through planning, taking an action (e.g. a new approach to teaching spelling), observing, monitoring and reflecting. This usually results in a reflective spiral that continues to move the researcher on in their thinking and practice. The aim is to involve the practitioner in improving their own practice.

**Control group**   Part of a sample that is compared with an experimental group (e.g. one group of children might be given an alternative method of phonics teaching and their progress compared with a group who carry on with their usual method – the latter is the control).

**Correlational studies**   Inquiries to discover relationships between variables and the strength of those relationships, in other words how likely would they be to appear again in another study (e.g. the extent to which reading ability is influenced by socio-economic factors).

**Empirical research**   Based on the observable evidence of data rather than on theory.

**Epistemology**   The study of the nature and characteristics of knowledge.

**Ethics**   A set of principles to ensure that researchers conduct their work in ways that are respectful and protective to all concerned (e.g. confidentiality, honest feedback).

**Ethnography**   Study of the structures of the social world.

**Experimental study**   Where comparisons are made between different approaches or interventions, usually by isolating a single variable for measurement.

**Grounded theory**   Theory that is developed from the collection, categorisation, defining and further testing of data. In other words the theory arises from the data rather than designing data collection to substantiate a theory.

**Hawthorne effect**   Where 'improvement' or effect of a new approach might be due to being a participant in a study (e.g. a new approach might be working because it has been prioritised by the participant teacher, or it has involved more time, or the teacher has greater enthusiasm) rather than because of the approach itself.

**Longitudinal study**   A study which is carried out over a longer period of time to measure long-term effects or changes.

**Methodologies**   The ways in which data are analysed, described and interpreted.

**Methods**   The ways in which data are collected.

**Non-empirical research**   Ideas and arguments constructed through theoretical ideas, literature searches, policy analysis, etc. rather than through new data.

**Paradigm**   A pattern or model. There are frequent references to 'research paradigms', meaning the different frameworks, methodologies and philosophies of research that now compete with and/or complement each other in today's educational research climate.

**Participant observation**   Observation in which the presence and influence of the researcher is acknowledged, and which may involve the researcher's interactions with the subjects of the research.

**Positionality**   The contexts and agendas of the researcher which may influence the design, interpretation or presentation of the research. It is always important for researchers to be aware of their own personal starting points as objectively as possible if partisanship is to be avoided. However, sometimes the involvement and influence of the researcher is an intentionally integral part of the study, in which case this should always be acknowledged in any discussion.

**Qualitative research**   The data are usually in word form rather than numbers, collected in ways such as interviews, observations, personal documents, etc. This means that studies are more likely to be small scale, but provide real depth of exploration that often provides new and unexpected findings. Based on the view that research takes place within social contexts that should be considered as part of the process research. Can be subjective. Quantities and coding of data can prove difficult although new approaches to this are being developed all the time.

**Quantitative research**   The data are usually numeric or categorical and can be analysed using statistical methods. Based on the presumption that knowledge is 'hard', objective and measurable. Derived from scientific research, and is also known as positivist research.

**Research Assessment Exercise (RAE)**   The Research Assessment Exercise is carried out every four years by the Higher Education Funding Council to assess the size of research grants to be allocated to institutions. Some argue that this process results in the inaccessible publication of research, because highly academic journals carry more 'points'. However, at the time of writing, the funding formula is under review, and there are indications to suggest that the impact and practical use of research is going to be an additional measurement factor in the next exercise.

**Sample**   Because it is not possible to measure whole populations of the groups we wish to study (e.g. every Year 3 pupil in Britain) we need to take a smaller sample. Sampling can be carried out in many different ways, e.g. random sampling, selective sampling, stratified sampling, systematic sampling, purposive sampling, etc. Appropriate sampling is a vital stage of even the smallest study because this affects considerably the extent to which conclusions can be drawn.

**Triangulation**   An approach by which two or more methods are used in order to compare and measure against each other for further validation of findings. This enables researchers to measure the same thing from different perspectives.

# Index